IRELAND'S WILD ATLANTIC WAY
A WALKING GUIDE

HELEN FAIRBAIRN

The Collins Press

FIRST PUBLISHED IN 2016 BY
The Collins Press
West Link Park
Doughcloyne
Wilton
Cork
T12 N5EF
Ireland

A CIP record for this book is available from the British Library.

Paperback ISBN: 978-1-84889-267-5
PDF eBook ISBN: 978-1-84889-566-9
EPUB eBook ISBN: 978-1-84889-567-6
Kindle ISBN: 978-1-84889-568-3

Design and typesetting by Fairways Design

Typeset in Myriad Pro

Printed in Poland by Białostockie Zakłady Graficzne SA

Contents

Route Location Map

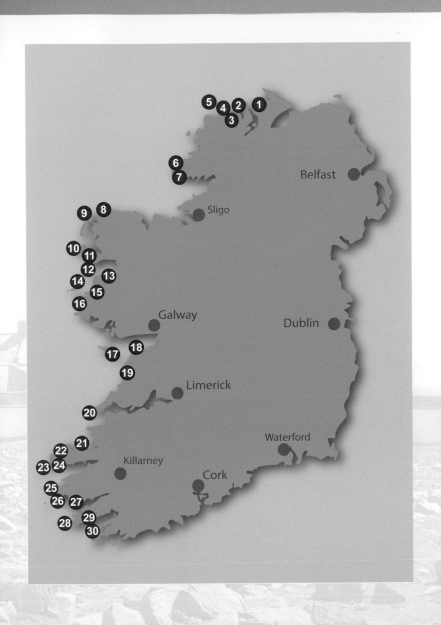

Belfast

Sligo

Galway

Dublin

Limerick

Waterford

Killarney

Cork

7

Quick-Reference Route Table

No.	Walk Name	Grade	Distance
1	Urris Lakes	3	7km
2	Melmore Head	4	12.5km
3	Ards Peninsula	2	7km
4	Tramore Strand	2	5km
5	Tory Island	2	11.5km
6	Glencolmcille	3	13km
7	Slieve League: Out-and-back from Bunglass	4	10km
	Slieve League: Traverse to Malin Beg	5	15km
8	Benwee Head	4	12km
9	Erris Head	2	5km
10	Achill Head & Croaghaun	5	13km
11	Minaun Heights	4	13km
12	Clare Island	4	15km
13	Croagh Patrick: Out-and-back from Murrisk	4	7km
	Croagh Patrick: Out-and-back via Ben Goram	4	8km
14	Inishturk	3	10km
15	Killary Harbour	3	6.5km
16	Omey Island	3	8km
17	Inisheer	3	10.5km
18	Black Head	4	14.5km
19	Cliffs of Moher	2	13km
20	Loop Head	3	10.5km
21	Magharee Peninsula	2	15km
22	Brandon Mountain	5	9km
23	Great Blasket Island	3	9km
24	Mount Eagle	3	8km
25	Bray Head	3	6km
26	Bolus Head	3	9km
27	Derrynane Mass Path	3	8km
28	Dursey Island	3	11.5km
29	Bere Island: Coomastooka Circuit	3	13km
	Bere Island: Lighthouse Loop	3	8km
30	Sheep's Head: Lighthouse Loop	3	4km
	Sheep's Head: The Poet's Way	3	12.5km

Hiker dwarfed by the Cliffs of Moher, the most celebrated stretch of cliffline in the country (see Route 19).

Intro

The Wild Atlantic
Stretching for over 2,5
south, it is really just a new
Ireland. With an emphasis on bold head
beaches and hidden coves, the route is a celebration of
treasures that lie along Ireland's Atlantic seaboard.

As with many beautiful landscapes, much of the best scenery lies off the beaten track, and can only be truly appreciated by those who explore on foot. There is simply no other way to reach the top of the country's highest cliffs or marvel at its most remote beaches except to walk there. The isolation of these places is part of their attraction. Standing at the tip of a chiselled headland, kilometres from the nearest road, walkers can appreciate the primeval atmosphere and raw power of nature in a way that most urban travellers cannot.

In this book, I have tried to gather a collection of routes that reflects the wide variety of scenery along the west coast, with the emphasis on wild and beautiful landscapes. There's a diversity of routes on offer, with walk durations ranging from two to six hours. There are easy routes along low, sandy shorelines, as well as tougher hikes to coastal summits. A handful of mountain routes require previous hillwalking experience, but most are less technical, crossing lower ground or following signed trails.

A trip along the Wild Atlantic Way is not just about the scenery, however: it is a journey through Irish culture and history too. Many of the routes described visit places with interesting background stories, and I have tried to highlight these wherever possible. Walks have been selected according to practical criteria also; circular routes have been prioritised over linear ones, and car parking and access issues have been carefully considered. The aim is to simplify the process of selecting a route that suits you, then help you complete the walk in confidence and with an enhanced appreciation of your surroundings.

Most people do not complete the entire Wild Atlantic Way in one trip. It would be a wonderful adventure to spend two months or more exploring the whole western seaboard from top to bottom, but practical considerations mean most walkers approach the area in smaller chunks. However much time you have, my hope is that you can to use this guide to discover the same inspirational places I have, and be rewarded for your effort by the same wonderful views and sense of awe at the natural world. The exhilaration and fulfilment that comes from exploring these hidden treasures should stay with you forever.

from north to south. But
voluted and indented part
gy and topography have
hes at least five times the
he land is so intricate it offers
ry – large peninsulas splitting into
ring further into spits and rocks, each shape
predecessor on a successively smaller scale.

The Atlantic coast is also the wildest part of the Irish seaboard. While the east coast is low and sheltered, the west is rugged and in places inaccessible, with sheer cliffs stretching unbroken for miles on end. The vast mass of the Atlantic Ocean is an ever-changing presence, sometimes benign but sometimes terrifying, as huge swells gather force across 3,000km of water before crashing onto the shore. The coast represents the front line in the battle between land and ocean, a constantly evolving landscape created by two elements at war.

The relentless impact of the waves sculpts the land, shaping rock and mountain alike. Millennia of erosion have left a tremendous variety of natural rock architecture, including sea stacks, arches, pinnacles and blow holes. Some formations are so tenuous it seems they will not survive the next storm. In other places entire hillsides have been chiselled into cut-away models of geological history, exposing distinctive rock strata that are twisted, folded and bedded into improbable patterns.

The cliffs themselves reach 600m high and are amongst the highest in Europe, surpassed only by Hornelen in Norway and Cape Enniberg in the Faroe Islands. Slieve League in Donegal (see p. 50) and Croaghaun on Achill Island (p. 65) vie for the title of tallest Irish sea cliff, depending on how you define the term 'cliff'. In other places the coastal precipice is not so high but it is more prolonged, stretching for miles with a thrilling vertical drop to the ocean below.

Not all of the west coast is steep and rocky, however – there are also plenty of places with a gentler, lower landscape. Sandy beaches are common, both in the form of wide holiday strands that are popular with families, and remote coves that barely see a soul all year. Ireland's beaches are every bit as beautiful and plentiful as in countries like Greece and Spain: it is just the climate that keeps the sun loungers at bay.

The coastal scenery does not finish with the mainland either. Ireland has hundreds of offshore islands, most of them located off the Atlantic coast. The largest island is Achill, in Mayo (see p. 65), while the most remote inhabited island is Tory, in Donegal (p. 40). Many of these apparently isolated outposts have a long history of human habitation, and though life has become increasingly untenable in recent times, at least forty still have a permanent population. Each island exudes a unique atmosphere, and many have stunning scenery to match. Together they form Ireland's final frontier, and are fascinating places for walkers to explore.

The coast is a great place for spotting wildlife. Remote cliffs and islands provide ideal nesting sites for a plethora of seabirds, including gulls, razorbills, guillemots, gannets, cormorants, shags and puffins. The nesting season generally lasts from April to August, and popular breeding sites buzz with avian activity during this time. Other habitats harbour different species. Oystercatchers gather on low, rocky shorelines, while sanderlings prefer to chase the waves on sandy beaches. Estuaries and tidal flats provide special havens too, with countless waders picking over the invertebrates exposed at each receding tide.

Ireland is a good place to see marine mammals. Almost a third of the earth's species of dolphins, porpoises and whales have been recorded here, and in 1991 the government set a European precedent when it declared Irish waters a whale and dolphin sanctuary. Large fin and humpback whales are best spotted off the coast of Cork and Kerry between July and October. The most common sighting along the coast as a whole is of a pod of dolphins leaping gracefully across the surface. Seals are also frequently seen, either hauled out on the rocks at low tide or feeding in shallow waters. The national seal census estimates the Irish seal population at over 10,000 animals, which includes half of Europe's grey seals.

There are sharks here too, thirty-nine different species of them. The biggest species present is the basking shark, which measures an average of 6m long and is the second largest fish in the world. These gentle giants are filter feeders, and during the summer you might be lucky enough to spot their dorsal fins gliding through the water as they sift for tiny crustaceans just below the surface.

Human History

The story of human settlement along the Atlantic coast is fascinating, and many of the routes in this book pass sites of historic relevance. The coasts were a focus of human activity from the time the first settlers arrived around 8000 BC. The interior of the country was heavily forested at that time, and it was often easier to get around by boat than across the land. With the seas providing a plentiful source of protein too, it made sense to establish communities along the shore.

Much of the earliest visible evidence of habitation stems from the Bronze Age, around 2500–500 BC. Several routes described here pass standing stones, burial mounds and other relics dating from that period. Two thousand years later, during the Iron Age, the construction of ring forts became popular. These are the most common type of archaeological remains found across Ireland, and near the coast they were often located at strategic vantage points. The fort of Cathair Dhúin Irghuis on Black Head (see p. 104) is a particularly well-preserved example.

The arrival of Christianity heralded a new era in Ireland, and there are many coastal landmarks associated with St Patrick and the latter-day saints. Ireland's holy mountain, Croagh Patrick (see p. 81), Glencolmcille (p. 45) and Brandon Mountain (p. 124) are just three of many sites linked to this period. By the eighth century the organisation of the Irish church was predominantly monastic. Omey Island (p. 95) is one example of the many places where monasteries were founded on islands or other remote coastal outposts, a practice that allowed monks to live free from distraction and persecution.

Vikings arrived in Ireland in AD 795, and though their reputation for violence is often overstated, they did wreak a certain amount of havoc along the coast. Dursey Island in Cork (p. 160) was once a Viking slave depot, while sheltered inlets such as Portdoon on Inishturk Island (p. 87) were settled because they provided ideal hiding places from which to launch their raids.

Many of the most obvious landmarks along the Wild Atlantic Way come from later periods of Irish history. Six of the walks in this book visit lighthouses, most of which were built by the British authorities during the nineteenth century. Another six routes pass tall, stone signal towers that are located on exposed headlands and coastal summits. These are part of a network of eighty-one towers that were constructed all around the coast between 1804 and 1806. Along with circular Martello towers and gun batteries, they formed part of the coastal defences set up to repel a possible French attack during the Napoleonic Wars. The towers could signal naval vessels at sea, as well as relay messages from one tower to another around the coast. The buildings stood two or three storeys high and were staffed by ten men, but after Napoleon's defeat at Waterloo in 1815 the threat of an invasion receded, and most of the towers were abandoned.

A similar network of buildings was established some 130 years later, during the Second World War. Instead of stone towers, a chain of eighty-three lookout posts was constructed around the coast. These small concrete bunkers were staffed by local members of the Coast Watching Service, a volunteer organisation created in 1939. The men operated on ten-hour shifts, and had to maintain continual observation of the sea and sky, tracking and logging all naval and air-force activity over a six-year period. The job must have been a bleak one, the only concession to comfort being a small fireplace. Telephones were added in 1940, but prior to this volunteers had to cycle to the nearest post office to relay crucial information – a long trip in many cases. Nonetheless the posts played an important role in wartime intelligence, recording more than 20,000 aircraft sightings over Ireland.

The Coast Watching Service was also responsible for building navigational signs on the ground near the lookout posts. The word 'EIRE' was written on the earth in large white stones, along with the identification number of the post. These signs served as daytime navigation aids for passing aircraft, and alerted pilots that they were flying over neutral Ireland rather than Britain. Surviving examples of the posts and signs can be seen on several walking routes along the Wild Atlantic Way, including at Loop Head in Clare (see p. 114) and Erris Head in Mayo (p. 61).

Walking Practicalities

Travelling along the west coast of Ireland has become easier with the development of the Wild Atlantic Way. Coast roads along the western seaboard are now marked with a chevron stripe, and an indication of whether you're travelling north or south along the route. In theory, if you joined the Wild Atlantic Way at one end of the country and followed it in its entirety, the signs would take you past every walk in this book.

Signage has also improved to towns, villages and points of interest along the west coast. There are numerous sites worthy of exploration, but fifteen locations have been deemed so spectacular they have been designated as Signature Discovery Points, or 'unmissable sights of the Wild Atlantic Way'. Not all these focal points are conducive to walking, but this guide includes walks around the eight that are.

Seven island walks are also described, and these require a little extra planning to complete. All the islands have regular ferry or cable car services, though in the case of uninhabited islands such as Great Blasket, these only operate from Easter to September. Contact details for the relevant transport operators are listed with each route, but timetables are subject to change so always check for updated departure times before you travel. Transport services can be disrupted by bad weather, so make sure to check the forecast too. If conditions seem at all questionable, double-check with the operator the evening before travelling. All the routes can be completed as day trips from the mainland, though it is tempting to stay overnight to soak up that special island atmosphere. The more populated islands have small shops, but the safest approach is always to bring everything you need for the walk with you from the mainland.

The nature of coastal walking means that the tide can be a consideration on lower routes. You may be able to stride across a firm, sandy beach at low tide, but at high tide the beach is covered and you are forced onto the land above. For any route where tide is a factor, both low and high tide options are described in the text. If you have a choice, however, walking around low tide generally gives you more options for progressing along the coast.

Other routes pass along the top of steep cliffs. It is an exhilarating experience to walk along a cliff edge, with a gaping abyss to one side and the waves crashing against the rocks hundreds of metres below. Yet it goes almost without saying that such exposure includes an inherent danger. Few cliff edges are fenced or protected in Ireland, and it is often up to walkers to exercise their own judgement in terms of safety. The best advice is to stay well back from the edge, be particularly aware of seaward-facing slopes if the ground is wet or slippery, and avoid cliff routes altogether in strong winds.

Around half the routes described are signed either completely or in some significant way. The most common form of signage is a series of waist-high posts, with arrows that point you in the right direction. The remaining walks cross open ground, and here you must rely on your own skills for route-finding. Walk descriptions give clear guidance to keep you on the correct route, and there might be informal paths on the ground to help you. The advantage of coastal walking is that the sea provides a constant point of reference, and many of the featured routes are relatively straightforward in terms of navigation.

There are just six routes that I would consider proper hillwalks. These are fabulous routes, but best left to confident walkers with previous mountain experience. All the normal mountain precautions apply, and you should carry an OSi map and compass to complete these walks in safety.

When to Walk

The walks in this guide can be completed all year round, though the season will have a significant impact on your experience. The coastal landscape changes considerably depending which time of year it is. Late spring and early summer are the most colourful periods, when coastal flowers like thrift and sea campion are in bloom. Seabirds gather at nesting sites in their thousands, and there's more human activity too, as beaches fill up with holidaying families.

The warmest months are July and August, when average daily temperatures reach 18 °C. This is the peak time for visitors along the Wild Atlantic Way, and you are likely to have company on your walks. It is also one of the best times to go island-hopping because ferry services are less likely to be disrupted by bad weather, and some ferries only run during the summer months.

By winter the flowers have gone and the bird ledges are empty. Some of the most popular areas, like the Cliffs of Moher, remain busy, though if you head to the more remote routes you may well have the scenery to yourself. January and February are the coldest months, when daytime temperatures average 6 °C and night-time temperatures often drop below freezing. There may be one or two modest falls of snow along the coast each winter, but these rarely last more than a few hours at sea level. Up on the peaks, however, snow may linger for a week or more. Wind chill is perhaps the biggest danger to walkers at this time, and several layers of insulation are needed to keep warm.

The ocean also becomes more agitated during the winter. The first big autumn swells usually hit the west coast around October, and storms can remain a regular occurrence right through to spring. These storms bring waves up to 20m high crashing into shore, especially in places where the continental shelf lies close to land. You should avoid all coastal walks in these conditions, because the spray and air gusts reach far higher again, and there have been several incidents where people have been swept off the rocks and have perished.

The Atlantic Ocean is the dominant influence on Ireland's climate as a whole, with the warm currents of the North Atlantic Drift keeping sea and air temperatures relatively mild. Prevailing winds come from the west or south-west and most rain falls as soon as the clouds meet land, so the Atlantic coast does receive almost a third more rain than the east. Winter is generally wetter, but there are still at least ten days with rain during most of the summer months. Rainfall is often short-lived, but the moral is that it is advisable to be prepared for showers in all seasons, even on apparently sunny days in summer.

As well as the climate and visitor numbers, another seasonal consideration for walkers is the amount of daylight. In mid December the sun rises around 8.40 a.m. and sets soon after 4 p.m., giving just seven and a half hours of daylight. By mid June, the sun sets at 10 p.m. and there are seventeen hours of daylight. It is quite possible to start a six-hour walk after lunch and still finish with light to spare.

Maps

The maps in this book provide accurate, scaled representations of each route and its surrounds, and provide sufficient guidance to complete most of the walks. The only exception is the mountain routes, where I recommend that you carry an additional small-scale map.

The long-established, standard reference for Irish walkers is the Ordnance Survey of Ireland (OSi) 1:50,000 *Discovery* series. These maps are of a high standard and cover the entire Wild Atlantic Way. Some sheets are also available with a waterproof covering.

OSi also produces the *Holiday* series, a range of four 1:250,000 touring maps that are handy for travelling along the west coast in general.

Local maps for the area you are in are widely available from bookshops, newsagents, tourist outlets and outdoor shops.

Useful Contacts

Listed below are the contact details of various service providers that might be of assistance to walkers on the Wild Atlantic Way.

Emergencies Dial 999 or 112 for all emergency services, including mountain rescue and coastguard.

Weather Forecasts The Irish Meteorological Service provides a two-day online weather forecast for Ireland at www.met.ie. The BBC offers a five-day forecast for the UK and Ireland at www.bbc.co.uk/weather/2635167.

Tide Times One of the best online resources for tide times is www.easytide.com. Select the closest spot on the map to your location to see a seven-day tide chart. Times and heights are given for both low tides (LW) and high tides (HW). Ireland has the same daylight saving hours as the UK, so between the end of March and the end of October you should use the dropdown menu to add one hour to the times.

Maps To buy walking maps online, go to www.osi.ie.

Signed Walks Ireland has many more signed walking routes than the ones recommended in this book. Use the interactive map at www.irishtrails.ie to see a wider selection of routes from each county.

Mountain Walks A great resource for Irish hillwalkers is www.mountainviews.ie. This website provides practical details about all Ireland's mountains, with walkers' comments detailing different routes up each peak.

Wild Atlantic Way For more general information about travelling and staying along Ireland's west coast, see www.wildatlanticway.com.

Using This Guide

This guide consists of thirty route descriptions covering what I consider the best one-day walks along the Wild Atlantic Way. Four of the walks also offer the choice of long or short alternative circuits. All the routes were checked in 2015, and descriptions were correct at that time.

Some of the walks are accessible by public transport, but you will need your own vehicle to reach the more remote excursions. The majority of the walks are circular in format, though there is one linear trip along the Cliffs of Moher, which uses public transport to return to the starting point. All the routes are located beside or very close to the coast, and virtually all the walking takes place across open ground or along footpaths and tracks. Road sections have been kept to a bare minimum, and main roads have been avoided completely.

Grading

Grades have been included to give an indication of the overall difficulty level, 1 being the easiest and 5 the hardest.

Grade 1 Relatively short walks on well-graded, constructed paths. Surfaces are firm underfoot and there is no significant ascent or descent. Routes are signposted throughout.

Grade 2 Routes still follow signed paths, but these might not be constructed underfoot. Some sections cross rougher ground or open countryside. There are no serious navigational difficulties but routes may involve up to 200m of vertical ascent.

Grade 3 Walks in this category are largely signed, but most paths are informal in nature, and there may be some sections across open, pathless terrain. Where there are no signs, route finding should be relatively straightforward in good conditions. There may be up to 500m of ascent and terrain can be rough underfoot.

Grade 4 Longer cross-country or mountain excursions with up to 750m of ascent. Ground can be very rough underfoot and any paths are informal in character. There are no signs so navigational skills are required throughout. Previous experience of independent walking is recommended.

Grade 5 The longest, most strenuous hillwalks fall into this category. Routes may visit multiple summits, last at least five hours and involve over 750m of ascent. Good stamina, solid navigational skills and previous hillwalking experience are all required to complete these routes in safety.

Sketch Maps

Every walk description is accompanied by a map that shows the route and surrounding terrain. The maps are accurate, scaled representations of the area, and can be relied on for navigational purposes. They provide sufficient guidance to complete most of the routes in the book, which means you will not have to buy the OSi sheet for every route you take on. The only exception is the mountain walks. The risk of getting lost in the mountains in poor weather means it is best to carry an additional map here that shows a wider area. For these routes I recommend that you carry the full OSi sheet, and a compass to assist with navigation should the weather turn bad.

All walks with more than 100m of ascent also include a height chart, allowing you to see the vertical profile of the route at a single glance.

Equipment

Boots are required for all walks unless the route description advises otherwise. Another general rule of walking in Ireland is that you should always be prepared for adverse weather. In the mountains in particular, warm and waterproof clothing is essential, even on an apparently sunny day.

Carry plenty of food and water, and a mobile phone. Be aware, however, that mobile coverage along the Wild Atlantic Way varies from very good to non-existent in more remote areas. Do not rely on being able to get a connection whenever you need it.

Responsible Walking

Many of the walking routes described in this book depend on the goodwill of landowners for their existence. Inconsiderate behaviour by walkers can lead to access being withdrawn and apparently established routes being lost. The main cause of contention is dogs. It is at the discretion of landowners whether they give permission for walkers to take dogs onto their land or not. Given the prevalence of sheep farming in Ireland, it comes as no surprise that dogs are generally banned. Damage to farm fences and walls, inconsiderate parking and litter are some of the other reasons why walkers become unpopular with landowners.

Inconsiderate outdoor behaviour can also have a negative impact on the environment and on other people's enjoyment of the area. Leave No Trace Ireland is a network of organisations that promotes responsible recreational use of the outdoors. It has designed a programme to help walkers and other outdoor enthusiasts understand the impact of their activities and to value the natural environment. For full details of the principles involved, please see www.leavenotraceireland.org.

One of the ruined cottages along the old famine relief road beside Killary Harbour,
County Galway (see Route 15)

ROUTE 1
Urris Lakes

Grade:	3
Time:	2–3 hours
Distance:	7km (4½ miles)
Ascent:	340m (1,120ft)
Map:	OSi 1:50,000 sheet 3

Climb a rugged hillside to reach two hidden lakes, enjoying wonderful coastal views across remote Lenan Bay.

Start & Finish: The walk starts and finishes at a small parking area at the back of Lenankeel beach (grid reference: C307437). Begin by heading to the town of Buncrana, County Donegal. From here, follow the Wild Atlantic Way signs north, past Dunree Head and over Mamore Gap. Take care descending down the north side of Mamore Gap as there are several very steep hairpin bends. At the bottom of the hill, turn left at a crossroads. Just over 1km later, this minor road turns sharp right beside a cluster of buildings. The parking area lies on the left just 50m beyond the bend, and is marked by a small map board. The car park may fill up at peak times, but further informal parking spaces can be found a short distance north along the road.

This beautiful hillwalk visits two secluded lakes on the northern slopes of the Urris Hills, on the Inishowen Peninsula. The western peaks of this rugged mountain chain drop directly to the sea, providing fabulous coastal views to Fanad Head and the mountains of north Donegal. The route starts and finishes at a remote, sandy beach at the back of Lenan Bay, and it is easy to spend extra time exploring the beach either before or after the walk.

The circuit is short but varied, with interesting terrain throughout. It is also fully signed, with purple arrows marking the way. Much of the route is spent along obvious mountain tracks, though the upper section around the lakes follows a worn path across open mountainside. At the very highest point the waymarks are slightly spread out and the path is not overly conspicuous, so care is needed here in misty conditions.

The walk has a poignant note too. At the western tip of the route, beyond Lough Fad, you descend into a broad valley. This valley marks the final resting place of a British Wellington bomber, which crashed here on Good Friday 1941, during the Second World War. The aircraft was returning from convoy escort patrol duty in the Atlantic, heading back towards Limavady airfield. Heavy mist reduced the visibility and the pilot became disorientated, crashing into this hillside and killing all six crewmen on board. Pieces of wreckage and a small

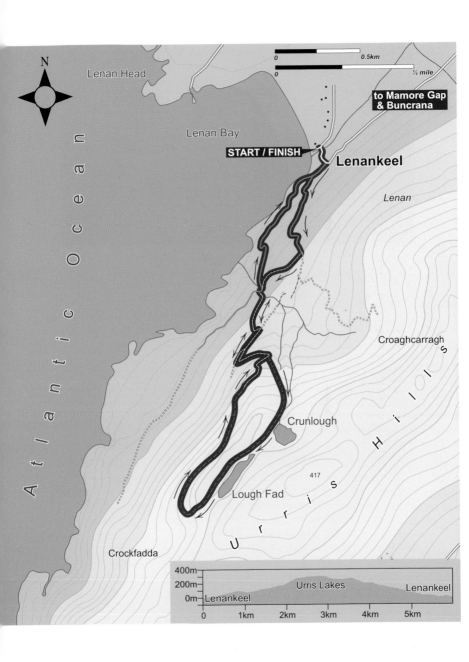

Crunlough lies tucked beneath rugged mountain slopes.

cross still mark the site of the accident, though they can be hard to find amongst the rocks and heather.

The Walk

From the parking area, head back to the road and turn right. Walk along the tarmac for 150m, passing a large shed. Now turn right beside a marker post and join a stony track. Pass through a gate and begin to climb steeply along the track. A short distance later you arrive at a fork. Keep left here – you will return along the right-hand track at the end of the circuit.

Continue climbing through a switchback and past a sheep pen. At the next junction turn right, passing though a couple of gates and continuing along the top of some old fields enclosed by stone walls. Already there are excellent views back to the north across Lenan Bay.

Beyond the old field enclosures, the track descends to reach another junction. Keep left here and head across a small footbridge to another junction. Turn left again and follow the track steeply uphill, climbing through a series of wide switchbacks. Where the track begins to peter out, look out for a waymark that indicates the start of a boggy footpath on the left.

The path strikes out across open mountainside, with wooden walkways in place to help you across the muddiest sections. Climb through a broad gully alongside the small stream that drains Crunlough lake, which remains hidden from view in the corrie above.

After another few minutes of effort you emerge onto the northern shore of Crunlough, a circular gem of a lake tucked beneath rugged and brooding mountain slopes. It is tempting to take a break here on the lakeshore to soak up the full atmosphere of the place.

When you're ready, follow the waymarks south-west, and in another few hundred metres you will see the long, narrow waters of Lough Fad down to the left. Climb onto a broad, rocky ridge that runs parallel to the lake's southern shore. Be careful here as the ground is scattered with sharp, ankle-turning rocks.

Continue south-west along the ridge, past a couple of rock cairns and some curious marble boulders. As the ridge ends, take time to savour the stunning views west across Lough Swilly to the Fanad Peninsula and the mountains of north Donegal. On a clear day the quartzite pyramid of Mount Errigal is prominent beyond the hump of Muckish Mountain, while the whitewashed walls of Fanad Lighthouse stand out to the north-west.

Descend steeply along a peaty trail, still heading south-west for a short distance, then swinging a full 180° to the right and heading back north-east. The route now makes its way along a broad, flat terrace with steep slopes above and below. At the end of this terrace, negotiate a short, steep descent that is eroded and awkward in places.

The path climbs again for a short distance, then brings you to the end of the track you followed on the outward leg of the walk. Keep left at the junction where the mountain path heads to Crunlough, and descend back through the switchbacks. Keep right at the next junction and recross the little footbridge. At the following junction the walk diverges from the outward route; turn left here and begin to follow a lower track down the hillside.

The descent back towards Lenankeel is very enjoyable, with more fabulous views across the low cliffs that fringe the southern side of the bay. Keep left at the next junction and retrace your initial steps through the gate to the road. Turn left here and complete the short distance back to the car park.

The route includes excellent views over Lenan Bay.

ROUTE 2

Melmore Head

Grade:	4
Time:	4–5 hours
Distance:	12.5km (8 miles)
Ascent:	200m (660ft)
Map:	OSi 1:50,000 sheet 2

With majestic Boyeeghter Strand as its centrepiece, the circuit of Melmore Head is one of Donegal's finest coastal walks.

Start & Finish: The route starts and finishes at Trá na Rosann car park, on the western side of Melmore Head (grid reference: C118420) in County Donegal. Approach the area via the R245, passing through the villages of Milford and Carrickart. As you leave Carrickart, take a right turn onto the R248, signed for Downings. Roughly 2km later you come to a junction. Continue straight ahead here, onto a minor road signed to Melmore Head. Follow this road for 6km, until it descends onto a flat expanse of machair. Turn left at the start of the flat area, following a sign for Trá na Rosann. The large car park is located at the end of this road.

Melmore Head lies at the north-west tip of the Rosguill Peninsula. An apparently diminutive finger of land, the eastern shore of the headland is low and softened by a succession of sandy beaches, while the west coast is wilder, punctuated by deep inlets and rugged hills. The beaches range from long, sweeping strands to tiny coves, and amongst it all is the grandeur of Boyeeghter Strand, one of the most dramatic beaches on the entire Irish coastline.

The route begins with 1.5km of road walking, but after that the terrain is almost exclusively natural, crossing beaches, dunes and grassy hills. As with many coastal walks, the exact route sometimes depends on the height of the tide; at low water you can stride easily across firm sand, while high tide may force you onto the land above. The toughest section is kept to the end – a steep ascent to the 163m summit of Crocknasleigh. The views more than justify the effort, however, and you will finish the day delighted to have explored the charms of this little-visited corner of Donegal.

A word of warning: do not underestimate the time required to complete this route. The land here is so fragmented you will cover several times the distance that first seems apparent from the map. Of course, it is possible to cut a few corners along the way, but make sure to allow at least four hours to explore the headland fully.

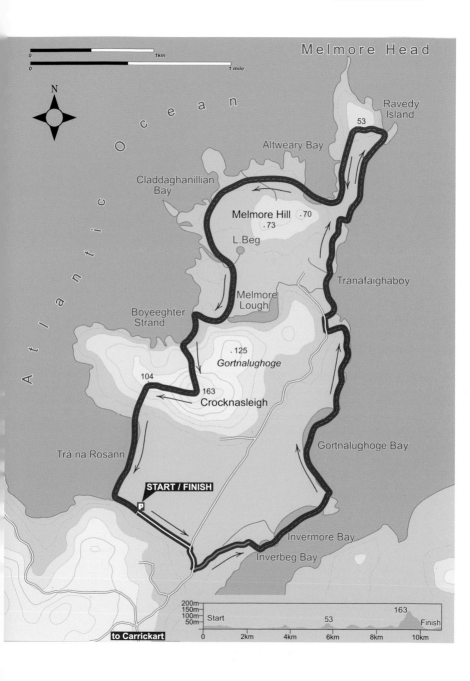

Melmore Head

Ravedy Island

Altweary Bay

Claddaghanillian Bay

Melmore Hill .70
.73

L.Beg

Tranafaighaboy

Melmore Lough

Boyeeghter Strand

.125
Gortnalughoge

104

163
Crocknasleigh

Gortnalughoge Bay

Trá na Rosann

START / FINISH

P

Invermore Bay

Inverbeg Bay

to Carrickart

Atlantic Ocean

N

0   1km
0   1 mile

53

200m
150m
100m
50m   Start   53   163   Finish
       0   2km   4km   6km   8km   10km

Beautiful Boyeeghter Strand is one of the last beaches visited on the route.

The Walk

Begin by walking south-east, back along the approach road to the car park. Turn right when you reach the main road, then turn left 200m later, just past a stone plaque for Dún Dubáin. Follow this lane for 500m, past several houses, to the end of the road. Now continue straight ahead onto a grassy footpath, descending through two pedestrian gates to reach a sandy cove known as Inverbeg Bay.

The route turns left here, and essentially follows the coastline all the way around Melmore Head and back to the car park. The first half of the route is particularly well endowed with beaches, and you will find yourself walking either along the sand, over low, grassy headlands between the beaches, or along dune trails just above the shore.

After Inverbeg Bay, pass over a low headland to reach a longer beach at Invermore Bay. Another grassy promontory then gives access to Gortnalughoge Bay, a particulary beautiful, curving beach that contains the longest continuous stretch of sand on the route.

Head across the sand to low rocks at the northern end of Gortnalughoge Bay. The best route over the next section depends on the height of the tide. At low tide you can follow the sand around a series of three small coves, each with its own helping of golden sand and turquoise water. At high tide some of these coves are cut off by the sea, and the best option is to follow a path through the dunes for 200m, or until you can return to the shore.

After the third cove the shoreline becomes rockier, so keep to a path at the edge of the dunes. Pass over a wooden stile in a fence, then climb slightly as the coast turns north-west. The coastal route is soon barred by a combination of a deep inlet and a tall metal fence around a bungalow. Turn left beside the fence and follow it through long grass for 100m to reach the road. Turn right here and follow the tarmac for 150m, until you can return to the shoreline at the beach of Tranafaighaboy.

At the northern end of Tranafaighaboy, head left between two mobile homes to reach a track. This will help you avoid the next awkward stretch of shoreline. A barrier across the track prevents motor traffic from proceeding further, but pedestrians are welcome. Follow the track north through the caravans for roughly 200m.

You are now at the narrow neck of dune that connects Melmore Head to the main peninsula, and again there are two options depending on the tide. At low tide, drop east onto a beach, then follow the shoreline north towards the small white lighthouse on Ravedy Island. Once here you can even descend a flight of steps and cross a causeway to visit the rocky islet itself. At high tide the coastal route is often covered by water. In this case, follow the track until it swings left, then continue straight ahead onto a grassy path. Turn right at a path junction and climb over a stile beside a metal gate. You are now on open ground on top of the headland, and can begin an anticlockwise circuit towards Ravedy Island, which will be detached from the mainland at this point.

From Ravedy Island, climb west along a faint path up the grassy slope. This brings you to the remains of an old signal tower at the 58m summit of Melmore Head. The coastal views are extensive: on a clear day you can look east across the rugged Fanad Peninsula to Malin Head, Ireland's most northerly point. To the west the 200m-high cliffs of Horn Head can be seen across the mouth of Sheephaven Bay.

Looking across Melmore Head from the top of Melmore Hill.

Descend south from Melmore Head, heading along the west coast, back towards the narrow neck of dune. Recross the stile and drop onto the cliff-backed beach in Altweary Bay. If the tide is low enough you can walk straight across the beach and scramble up the rocks at its western end. At high tide you may have to climb over Melmore Hill (70m), a stiff little climb rewarded by excellent views, from where you can descend north-west to rejoin the coastal route.

The next stretch of coastline is flat and rocky with a conspicuous grassy headland commanding attention. Pass a storm beach and small enclosure before turning south again into Claddaghanillian Bay, where an altogether wilder scene is revealed. Several shattered fingers of rock thrust into the Atlantic, backed by the rugged cliffs beneath Crocknasleigh.

The route now veers inland to circumvent a long, narrow inlet. From here it is worth heading south to see Melmore Lough, a beautiful, L-shaped lake that nestles beneath steep slopes. From the western end of this lough, follow a high stone wall west across a short rise, where a gap in the wall lets you cross onto a promontory. Your breath will now be taken away by the sudden view over Boyeeghter Strand. This is surely one of the wildest and most beautiful beaches in Ireland, its striking golden sand backed by dark cliffs and pounded by lines of swell. A more sinister local name for the beach is The Murder Hole, an apparent reference to an incident in the nineteenth century when a woman was pushed to her death from the cliff above.

Boyeeghter Strand, also known as The Murder Hole.

At high tide or in stormy weather you may not be able to reach the main strand, and will have to climb south across the hill above the beach. At other times, cross back through the gap in the wall and head north for 100m, where you can descend through the dunes to the sand. If the conditions are right, be sure to visit the cave at the back of the main beach.

Leave the beach via a steep grassy gully at its southern end. Continue climbing the steep slope above to reach a superlative viewpoint at the top of Crocknasleigh, some 163m above the sea. The climb is strenuous, but if you pause for a rest you can enjoy remarkable views back along the coast. On a clear day the top of Crocknasleigh provides a fitting finale to the route, giving a fabulous 360° panorama of north Donegal.

To descend back to the start, head west towards point 104m, then drop south onto Trá na Rosann. Cross to the southern end of the beach, then head left up a sandy path and wooden boardwalk, which brings you back to the car park.

Ards Peninsula

Grade:	2
Time:	2–3 hours
Distance:	7km (4½ miles)
Ascent:	140m (460ft)
Map:	OSi 1:50,000 sheet 2

This highly enjoyable, easy route explores a pleasant mixture of woodland and beach-strewn coastline.

Start & Finish: The route starts and finishes at Ards Friary, at the south-eastern tip of Ards peninsula (grid reference: C087346) in County Donegal. Access to the area is via the N56. One kilometre north of Creeslough village, turn east and follow signs to the friary. The final part of the road makes a one-way loop, and there is a large car park in front of the friary itself. Other facilities include public toilets and a weekend coffee shop.

From a brief glance at the map, Ards peninsula seems rather modest. It lies tucked away at the back of Sheephaven Bay, dwarfed between the bolder promontories of Melmore Head and Horn Head. In fact Ards loses and regains its status as a headland with each procession of the tide. At low tide the surrounding river estuaries are naked sand flats cut by meandering ribbons of water, then a few hours later the ocean returns and surrounds the peninsula, stretching down for 3km or more on either side.

Despite its humble dimensions, the pleasure of walking at Ards should not be underestimated. This is a fantastic route, and the coastal scenery is every bit as beautiful as that offered by more challenging outings. There might not be any towering cliffs, but there are 4km of sandy bays separated by rocky headlands, and a wonderfully peaceful atmosphere throughout.

The route makes a circuit around the northern tip of Ards. It begins by following woodland tracks that cross over the spine of the peninsula, then returns along a series coastal paths. Ascent is modest and the terrain is firm throughout, so this route is suitable for most people, including families. There are two possible starting points: either the forest service car park on the northern side of the peninsula (for which you will need €5 in coins to operate the entrance barrier), or Ards Friary, on the southern shore. The circuit described here begins at the friary, if only to take advantage of the free parking, lack of closing time, calm atmosphere, and coffee shop (open on weekends).

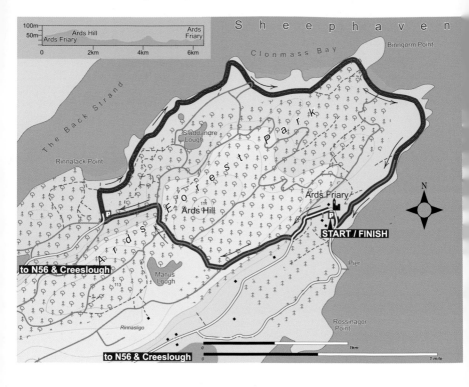

The Walk

Ards Friary dates from 1708, and is home to a small community of Franciscan Capuchin monks. Though the dwindling number and advancing age of the friars meant closure seemed imminent in 2006, the centre has now been revitalised and hosts regular spiritual retreats and conferences all year round.

With your back to the friary, begin by walking to the right, back up the access road you arrived on. Look for the second track on the right, which comes 500m along the wooded lane. Turn into the forest here, climbing gently past mature beech trees.

After 700m along the track, look out for a junction. The main trail continues straight ahead, while on the right, a side trail has been blocked to vehicles with a mound of soil and a makeshift fence. Turn right here, climb over the heap of soil, and follow a footpath into the forest beyond.

Before long you arrive at the corner of a larger track, which is marked with red and blue symbols indicating two of the forest walks. Continue straight ahead along the track, following a sign for the car park. The route begins to descend now, still passing through mixed woodland. Over the years this part of the peninsula has been variously planted and cleared into patchwork stands of broadleaved and coniferous trees. Areas currently felled are being replanted with native broad-leaved species, reflecting the fact that Ards is now essentially a recreational rather than a commercial woodland.

Continue straight ahead at the next junction, then take the following left, heading all the while in the direction indicated for the car park. When you meet the paved access road, turn right, pass the toilet block, and head straight across the car park. The children's play area is straight ahead, but you should

The route begins by following a forest track past mature beech trees.

turn right onto a paved footpath signed with the orange symbols of the Sand Dune Trail.

You have now reached the coast, which you follow all the way around the tip of the headland and back to the start. Pass around the back of a beach and continue across the dunes on a delightful section of wooden boardwalk. At low tide, the wide sand flats of the Back Strand will be

The Sand Dune Trail involves a delightful section of wooden boardwalk.

A series of sandy coves leads round to the cliffs of Binngorm Point.

exposed, and you may well see flocks of eager, long-billed waders probing the bay in search of hidden invertebrates.

When the boardwalk comes to an end, turn right onto a sandy path. This turns into a grassy trail that runs along the edge of the dunes, just above a beach. If you prefer, there's also plenty of opportunity to drop down onto the beach and walk along the sand itself. This is Clonmass Bay and the scenery is fantastic, an intricate mix of golden sand, blue sea and rugged hummocks, with the village of Downings visible across Sheephaven Bay ahead.

If you have chosen to walk along the dunes, join a gravel trail and turn left for 80m. Here you should drop onto the sand, now following the white markers of the Marine Trail. Follow the beach to its eastern end, where a short, steep climb brings you to the top of the headland. Here you're met by another fabulous view. To the east, a series of sandy coves are separated by jagged fins of rock, all leading round to the cliffs of Binngorm Point.

Follow a grassy path around the headland, then return to the gravel trail beside a stone shelter. Turn left onto the gravel, pass around a corner, then turn left again onto a smaller footpath marked by the blue symbols of the Binngorm Trail. Climb over a series of steps and switchbacks to reach the top of the headland, where the path weaves through a copse of twisted trees.

As you exit the vegetation you find yourself high above the sea, with open ocean visible at the mouth of Sheephaven Bay to the north. The deep water below the headland is located at the mouth of two estuaries, and is rich in nutrients. This attract shoals of fish, and in the summer you may well see gannets, Arctic terns and other seabirds performing high-speed aerial manoeuvres as they dive-bomb into the waves below.

The path drops down into a sandy cove sheltered between the twin headlands at the tip of the peninsula. Cross the beach to its opposite corner, then climb to the left to reach the top of the next headland. Here you meet another gravel trail. Turn left and follow this path around the promontory, gradually descending to the southern shore of the peninsula, with the 5km sweep of Tramore ('Big Beach') visible across the estuary ahead.

Keep straight ahead along the path, then pass through a stone gateway into the grounds of Ards Friary. A final stretch of path leads above the shore and through some trees to reach a white metal gate. Turn right here to return to the friary and coffee shop, which is unfortunately open on weekends only.

Ards Capuchin Friary at the start and finish of the walk.

ROUTE 4

Tramore Strand

Grade:	2
Time:	1½–2 hours
Distance:	5km (3 miles)
Ascent:	160m (525ft)
Map:	OSi 1:50,000 sheet 2

This short circuit takes you through a vast, protected dune system to a hidden 2km-long beach.

Start & Finish: The route starts and finishes at a car park just north of Hornhead Bridge (grid reference: C008376). Begin by heading along the N56 to the village of Dunfanaghy, in northern Donegal. At the western end of Dunfanaghy Main Street, turn north, following signs to Horn Head. Drive across Hornhead Bridge and around 80m later, turn left up a gravel lane signed to the looped walk parking area. The car park is on the left some 200m later, and provides ample space for around fifteen vehicles.

Swathes of rosebay willowherb carpet the machair during the summer.

This is one of the shortest and easiest walks in this book, but it takes you past some unforgettable coastal viewpoints and visits one of the most beautiful beaches in Ireland. The only way to reach 2km-long Tramore Strand is by boat or by foot, but the inaccessibility of the bay only heightens its charm for those who make the effort to discover it.

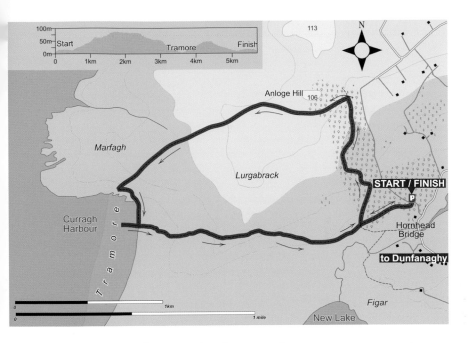

The walk is fully signed and crosses pleasant yet unconstructed surfaces throughout. It explores the neck of land at the southern end of the Horn Head Peninsula. Horn Head was still an island until as recently as the twentieth century, separated from the mainland by a narrow, tidal channel. During the First World War, large quantities of marram grass were harvested from the shore to provide bedding for animals. The unsecured sands drifted across the channel, which was finally blocked by a storm in 1917. This marked the end of Dunfanaghy's position as an important fishing port, but did create New Lake, which is now a wildfowl sanctuary.

It was once possible to extend this route into a longer trip that ran right around the coast of Horn Head, taking you past the 200m-high cliffs at the northern tip of the headland. Unfortunately, access issues mean this outing is no longer possible. At the time of writing a second signed walk was being developed, which will explore the most dramatic cliff scenery around the cliffs to the north. Known as the Coastguard Hill Loop, this 8km route should be complete by summer 2016, and will provide another fine option for walkers in the area. The route will start and finish at the northern end of the Horn Head road (grid reference: C014409), and is well worth checking out if you are in the area.

The Walk

From the car park, pass through the gate and follow a broad trail that heads west through the forestry plantation. After a few hundred metres you arrive at a junction near the edge of the trees, beside a small stream and information board. The route will return to this point at the end of the circuit. For now, follow a marker post that directs you to the right, onto a narrower, more informal trail.

Climb gently north through the forest for almost 1km. As the trees thin out into a clearing, the path swings back to the west. Leave the final, stunted trees behind, and head out into a vast area of marram grass and dune. This is Lurgabrack Sand Dunes, a large but delicate coastal habitat that is designated as a Special Area of Conservation. The dunes provide a haven for the cinnabar moth, and Greenland White-fronted Geese also spend the winter here.

The route across the dunes is very enjoyable, with firm terrain underfoot and a palpable feeling of space all around you. The trail begins by heading in a north-westerly direction, but gradually swings around to the south-west. There are views across the Pollaguill Valley to the north and the headlands at Marfagh to the west, with the Atlantic just visible beyond.

As the trail swings further south you get your first tantalising glimpses of the Donegal highlands, with the summits of Muckish, Errigal and the Aghlas visible over the sea of grass. Soon the coastline begins to reveal itself too, unveiled in order with the most distant landmarks first. The jagged outline of Tory Island provides the initial point of reference, followed by the cliffs of Bloody Foreland and Dooros Point. Finally the sweeping sands of Tramore Strand come into sight, more and more of the bay becoming exposed until you are standing at a turnstile on top of the low cliffs that form the northern boundary of the beach.

Pass through the turnstile and turn left onto a trail that runs along the clifftop and into the dunes behind the beach. A short, steep descent brings you down a sandy path to another gate and a trail junction. The signed route turns left here and heads inland, but it is well worth detouring to the right and passing through the gate to visit Tramore Strand itself. This beautiful,

Muckish Mountain rises above Lurgabrack sand dunes.

View along Tramore Strand from the low cliffs to the north.

golden sweep of sand is a wonderful place to linger; you can walk as far as you like along the beach, or simply perch on the rocks at its northern end to survey the wonderful coastline in front of you.

When you're ready, return to the trail junction and resume the circuit. The trail climbs steadily inland through another expanse of machair, dune and marram grass. As you gain elevation there are fine views across New Lake to the south. During the summer this area is carpeted with wildflowers, and includes species like bird's-foot trefoil and rosebay willowherb.

Pass over a ridge and descend steeply to a wide stretch of pan-flat machair. A few hundred metres later, cross a stream and re-enter the forest at the path junction you encountered at the start of the walk. Keep straight ahead this time, and follow the broad trail back to the car park.

A sandy trail leads through the marram grass of Lurgabrack.

ROUTE 5

Tory Island

This remote north-western outpost offers a spectacular coastline and unique island atmosphere.

Start & Finish: The route starts and finishes at the ferry pier on Tory Island (grid reference: B856464), County Donegal. Boat services are operated by **The Tory Island Ferry** (Tel: 074 9531 320 / 074 9135 061; www.toryislandferry.com). An adult return costs €26 from both Magheraroarty (35 minutes) and Bunbeg (90 minutes). There are daily services all year round, most of which allow at least four hours on the island, so it is quite feasible to complete the walk as part of a day trip. At the time of writing, boats depart from Magheraroarty at 11.30 a.m., and from Bunbeg at 8.45 a.m., but the best advice is always to check departure times before making your trip. Check the forecast before travelling too, as it is not uncommon for visitors to be stranded on the island during bad weather.

Magheraroarty (Machaire Uí Rabhartaigh) is reached by turning off the N56 onto the R257 at the western end of Gortahork, near Falcarragh. The road is signposted 'Coastal Route/Bloody Foreland'. As you arrive in Magheraroarty village, around 5km away, the pier is obvious at the bottom of a steep hill on the right (grid reference: B889334).

The storm-battered island of Tory (Oileán Thóraigh) lies 12km off the coast of Donegal, and is probably the most remote place to walk in Ireland. It also rates amongst the country's most evocative and intriguing locations, and is one of its smallest inhabited islands at just 5km long and 1km wide.

Separated from the mainland by the treacherous waters of Tory Sound, the island lies in the path of ferocious storms and heavy seas. In 1974, after an eight-week storm lashed the island without mercy, the government made plans for the permanent evacuation of Tory. Thankfully this did not happen, due in part to the efforts of Father Diarmuid Ó Peícín, who spearheaded a campaign to raise funds, create a proper ferry service, establish an electrical supply and more. A community of around 140 inhabitants still perseveres, and today the island is a central part of the Donegal Gaeltacht, and is renowned for its particular form of Ulster Irish.

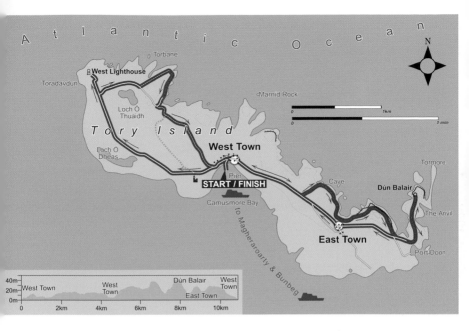

There are two main villages on Tory: West Town – where the ferry docks and most of the island's services and accommodation can be found – and East Town, which is a little more than a scattering of bungalows. During the summer months the island teems with birdlife, with all the usual coastal species supplemented by the largest concentration of corncrakes in Ireland. The distinctive call of this rare and elusive bird can often be heard around West Town. Like many of the island's birds it nests on the ground, however, and walkers should take great care where they tread if leaving paths and tracks during the breeding season (May to August).

The first, western half of this route follows the signs for the Tory Island Loop Walk. However, the signed trail fails to visit the eastern side of the island, and hence misses all the best scenery. The route described here includes a second loop to the

Colourful cottages in West Town.

Spectacular cliffs line the promontory of Dún Balair.

island's north-eastern tip. This is where you will find Tory Island's most dramatic coastline, with sheer cliffs and razor-sharp arêtes providing the undisputable highlight of the route. This section does take you along the top of steep drops, so take care near the edge and avoid the area in high winds.

The Walk

From the ferry pier, head up into the village of West Town. The village boasts two significant landmark monuments, both of which are visible as soon as you step off the boat. Above the main slipway is a twelfth-century Tau Cross, one of only two such T-shaped cruciforms in Ireland. A small distance away lies the ruin of a sixth- or seventh-century round tower. These two sites are all that remain of a monastery that was founded here by St Colmcille, but largely destroyed by English troops in the fifteenth century.

Pass the Tau Cross, then turn left and walk west along the road through the village. Before long you pass the round tower, then a small stone enclosure on the left known as Móirsheisear, or the Church of the Seven (although the name literally translates as 'Big Six'). This marks the grave of seven people – six men and one woman – who drowned when their currach capsized. The soil from the woman's grave is reputed to ward off rats; to this day the island is a rat-free zone, which helps explain its popularity with ground-nesting birds.

A short distance beyond Móirsheisear, turn left at a junction and follow the lane out towards Loch Ó Dheas. The road then swings north and heads for the lighthouse, which was built between 1828 and 1832 and is now fully automated. At the lighthouse gate, the route turns right and continues along a track. Before you leave, however, it is worth walking around the boundary wall to view the lighthouse from the western end. A small stone enclosure acts as a graveyard for eight bodies recovered from HMS *Wasp*, which sank close to Tory in 1884. This British navy vessel was on its way to Tory to collect overdue rents; since then, no rents have been paid on the island.

When you're ready, return to the track junction and turn left. The track is partially paved here by rough, granite cobbles. Pass Loch Ó Thuaidh, then turn left beside the ruins of a former barracks. A side loop takes you round a headland to a small wooden hut, which was once used by the English landscape artist Derek Hill. Follow the path around the coastline and past a small slipway to reach another junction, where you should turn left.

Follow the track back into West Town. The signed loop walk ends in the village, but this route turns left and heads south-east along the road towards East Town and Dún Balair. After a kilometre, leave the road and walk north-east to the cliffs, which are just a short distance away. Here you will find a large hole set back from the cliff edge, where the roof of a cave has collapsed. Follow the cliffs south-east around a deep inlet, then onto a wild promontory with stunning views east to Dún Balair.

Carefully descend the grassy slopes leading towards Port Doon, then cross over the narrow, grassy isthmus that connects Dún Balair with the rest of Tory. Turn north here and begin the steady climb up increasingly barren and rocky slopes to the cairn crowning the summit of Dún Balair. This is the highest spot on the island at 83m. The name translates to English as 'Balor's Fort', in reference to the one-eyed pre-Celtic god who was chief of the Fomorians. The summit provides a superlative viewpoint, with the whole of Tory laid out before you and the Atlantic heaving and pounding far below. Close to the top of Dún Balair is Leac na Leannán, or the Wishing Stone. It is said that those who stand on top of this curious pedestal of rock are granted a wish, though perhaps because it is so dangerous to do

The fabulous view over north Tory from the summit of Dún Balair.

West Lighthouse was built between 1828 and 1832.

so, you can also gain the privilege by throwing three stones, one after the other, onto the top.

Far to the south the distinctive profiles of Donegal's Derryveagh Mountains are ranged across the mainland horizon. Looking north you simply can't miss An Eochair Mhór (The Big Key), a huge, razor-thin blade of rock extending far out from the headland. It is capped by Tormore, and ranged along the arête are several fantastically weathered pinnacles known as Saighdiúirí Bhaloir, or Balor's Soldiers.

Unless you fancy tiptoeing out to Tormore, you have to turn around at Dún Balair and descend back towards Port Doon. From here it is simply a matter of joining the road and turning right, and walking back through East Town to the pier where you started.

West Town harbour and ferry pier.

ROUTE 6
Glencolmcille

Grade:	3
Time:	4–5 hours
Distance:	13km (8 miles)
Ascent:	500m (1,640ft)
Map:	OSi 1:50,000 sheet 10

The combination of ancient monuments and striking coastline makes this a memorable outing for any walker.

Start & Finish: The route starts and finishes at St Columba's Church, in the centre of Glencolmcille village (grid reference: G535849), County Donegal. Glencolmcille is located around 24km west of Killybegs along the R263. A small car park in front of the church provides space for around ten vehicles.

Glencolmcille is a place of unique character and other-worldly atmosphere, set amidst some of the country's wildest coastline. It is a remote spot that is steeped in history; human settlement dates back 5,000 years, and the village is surrounded by a remarkable number of Neolithic and Early Christian monuments. In many cases, former pagan sites have been given new meaning within the Christian faith. On 9 June each year, thousands of pilgrims still visit the area to pray at the fifteen ancient stations of the Turas, making a journey of religious pilgrimage around the village.

Glencolmcille is also surrounded by some of the most spectacular coastal and mountain scenery in Ireland. In addition to the religious pilgrims, well-informed hillwalkers have long been making the journey from here to the deserted village of Port, 6km north along the coast. In recent years, the development of several signed walking routes has simplified both access and route-finding in the area. The route described here is a 'mix and match' circuit that uses the Tower Loop, Drum Loop and Bealach na Gaeltachta – all of which are signed walking trails – as well as a stretch of open coastline, to complete a trip around the best sites and scenery in the region.

The terrain underfoot is a mixture of laneway, track and open hillside, and roughly three quarters of the walk is signed in some form. The route also passes along the top of exposed cliffs, so please take care near the edge.

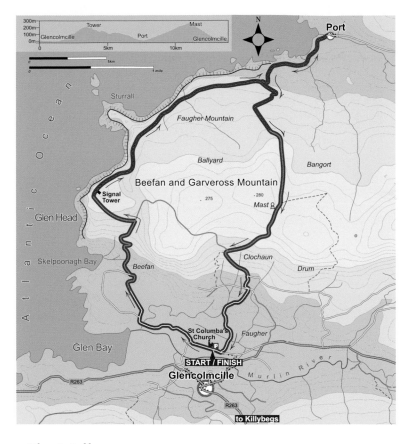

The Walk

The route starts at St Columba's Church. Despite his status as the village namesake, the association with St Columba remains something of a mystery, as there is no firm evidence of the saint actually being here. The first section of the walk follows the blue arrows of the Tower Loop, so begin by heading west along the road. After just 80m you reach the first antiquity of the day: a carved pillar set atop a rise on the right side of the road. This is one of the best cross-inscribed, Early Christian pillars in Ireland, and a set of stone steps provides access to let you explore the site.

Continue along the road for 50m, then turn right at the junction. This lane leads around a corner and along the sandy mouth of the Murlin River. Cross a bridge over a tributary stream, then turn right onto a smaller lane. Soon you pass Turas station No. 3 on the left – a small Mass rock beside a cairn.

The dramatic arête of Sturrall lies just north-east of the signal tower.

Continue along the lane towards a cottage, then veer right onto a grass boreen just in front of the house. Climb steeply to a junction with another lane and turn left. Roughly 80m later, turn through a gate on the right and begin to climb along a stone track. Colmcille's Well – Turas Station No. 7 – is signed to the right here, and consists of a court cairn with a well and an ancient stone image of Colmcille inside. It can be tricky to find, however, as it lies tucked into a hollow in the hillside.

Walker examining the Early Christian carved pillar near the start of the route.

The Napoleonic signal tower at Glen Head is remarkably intact.

Follow the track as it climbs up the open hillside. A series of switchbacks negotiates the steep terrain, but there are fantastic views south-west across Skelpoonagh Bay to distract you from the effort. At the top of the ascent the track forks. The main circuit of the Tower Loop heads to the right, while the signal tower is signed to the left. You should turn left, and climb more gently across peaty ground to reach the signal tower.

The tower is a huge, imposing stone structure, one of three Napoleonic watchtowers that grace the headlands around Glencolmcille. All three buildings were constructed between 1804 and 1806, though they were staffed for just a handful of years before being abandoned completely in 1815. The tower's vantage point is predictably impressive too. Beneath your feet the cliffs of Glen Head drop 200m to the Atlantic, while fabulous views extend along the shattered coastline in both directions.

Leave the signed loop walk here and begin to head north-east along the coast, following an informal path through the grass. A short distance beyond the signal tower, the dramatic arête of Sturrall thrusts into the sea, its white rock, curving spine and precipitous slopes making it one of the most distinctive coastal formations in Ireland.

Continue to follow the coast past the headland, taking care along the exposed cliff edge. Descend across a hollow, then veer inland (east) across a kilometre of rough, heather-covered ground. The view ahead is dominated by huge cliffs beneath Port Hill and the jumble of massive sea stacks in the bay below.

When you meet a bog track signed as part of the Bealach na Gaeltachta, turn left and make the final descent to Port. This village was deserted in the 1940s, and the ruined stone buildings combine with the awesome scenery to make it an extremely evocative place. In good conditions this is a great location for a break, and it is tempting to linger a while to explore the area in more detail.

When you're ready, turn around and return to the track you used on your outward journey. Follow the track as it climbs steadily for some 260 vertical metres to reach a communication mast at the barren summit of Beefan and Garveross Mountain. Cross straight over a junction at the top of the hill, then descend steeply along a lane, soon rejoining the route marked by the blue arrows.

Follow the road downhill towards the houses of Glencolmcille. Near the bottom of the slope, some slabs of rock in a small field are actually Mainnéar na Mortlaidh, a court tomb believed to date from 3000 BC. A short distance further along the road you will find Cloch Aonach (the Meeting Stone), a carved pillar with a hole near the top. In pagan times this was where people would get married, the union sealed when the couple joined fingers through the hole. The Christian practice involves walking around the stone three times and denouncing Satan. If the pilgrim achieves a state of grace, it should be possible to look through the hole and see paradise on the other side.

A short climb brings you to a T-junction at the end of the road. Turn right here to return to St Columba's Church, where the route began.

A jumble of massive sea stacks litter the coast around Port.

Slieve League

Out-and-back from Bunglass		Traverse from Bunglass to Malin Beg	
Grade:	4	**Grade:**	5
Time:	3½–4½ hours	**Time:**	4½–5½ hours
Distance:	10km (6 miles)	**Distance:**	15km (9½ miles)
Ascent:	500m (1,640ft)	**Ascent:**	570m (1,870ft)
Map:	OSi 1:50,000 sheet 10	**Map:**	OSi 1:50,000 sheet 10

This route over Donegal's most majestic sea cliffs is an Irish classic, with options including a simple out-and-back or a full traverse of the mountain.

Start & Finish: The main route starts and finishes at Bunglass car park (grid reference: G558757). To reach this point from Killybegs, head west along the R263. Pass through Carrick and Teelin, then turn right onto a steep road signed for Bunglass. Pass through a gate (be careful to close it behind you) and continue to the parking area at the end of the road.

The alternative, linear route finishes at a car park in Malin Beg (grid reference: G498800). To get there from Carrick, head north along the R263 for 4km, then turn left onto a minor road. Roughly 7km later, turn left again onto the R263, and continue to the car park at the end of the road.

View across the Slieve League cliffs from the Eagle's Nest.

Slieve League is home to some of the highest and most impressive sea cliffs in Europe, and is rightly celebrated as one of the Signature Discovery Points of the Wild Atlantic Way. Viewed from inland the first impression is of an unremarkable whaleback of a mountain, but move to the seaward side, and you cannot help but be awestruck by the scale of the cliffs that plunge dramatically into the ocean below. Thousands of years of wave action have eaten away at the mountain's south-western face, leaving sheer rock faces and precipitous slopes that stretch for 2km at over 500m high. It is a fantastic scene, and only Croaghaun on Achill Island can compete in terms of grandeur in Ireland.

The good news for walkers is that this is one of the most popular hillwalks in Donegal, and there are several well-trodden routes to the summit. The standard out-and-back approach leaves from the car park at Bunglass. If you can arrange transport logistics, however, the connoisseur's route is a full traverse of the mountain from Bunglass to Malin Beg. This trip extends far beyond the popular area at the start, and really makes the most of this fantastic coastline. Use either a second vehicle or a local taxi firm to arrange return transport.

Bear in mind, however, that this is not an easy walk – it has more in common with a mountain ascent than a lowland coastal route. There is a path constructed from stone slabs for the first stretch from Bunglass, but beyond that you will be following an informal trail up sometimes steep slopes. Much of the walk is spent alongside a sheer and unprotected drop, so please take great care near the edge. Avoid walking in poor visibility or strong winds, and make sure to carry the OSi map if you have decided to tackle the full traverse.

The Walk

Out-and-back from Bunglass

The route starts with a bang straight from Bunglass car park. If you have never been here before, the sudden sight of the cliffs falling half a kilometre into the ocean in front of you is utterly absorbing. Little wonder that this place is also known as Amharc Mór, which translates as 'Big View'.

Begin by taking a well-constructed flagstone path from the north-eastern corner of the car park. Pass a wooden viewing platform, and continue up the trail beyond. The path is maintained for the first section, where the number of passing feet is greatest.

Head north-east around the cliffs, climbing several flights of steps to reach the top of Scregeighter (308m). The path now becomes more informal in nature, though it remains obvious underfoot. Swing north-west and climb along the cliff edge to the Eagle's Nest (323m), where the drop to the ocean is almost vertical. The exposure here is impressive, but please exercise due caution.

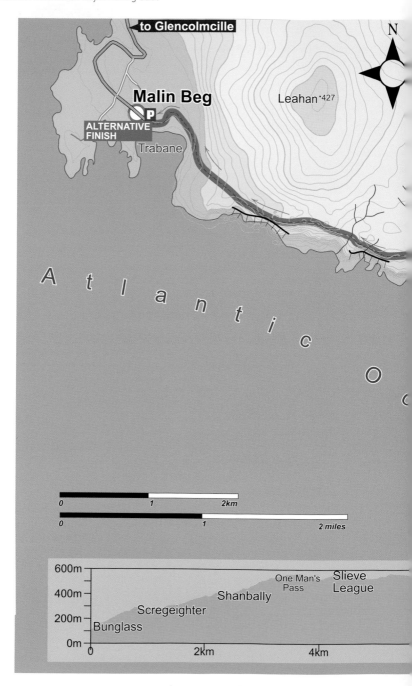

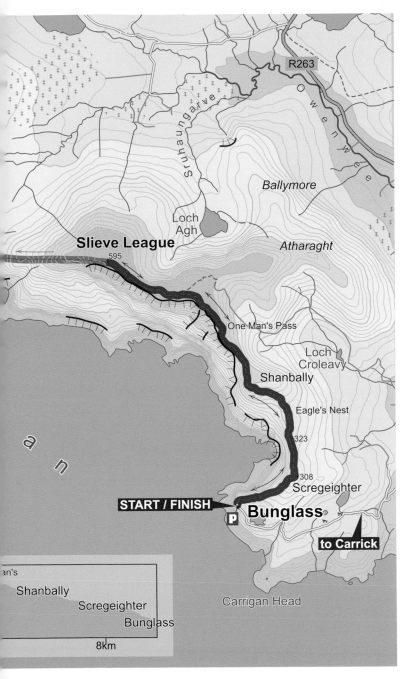

R263

O w e n w e e

S r u h a u n g a r v e

Ballymore

Loch
Agh

Slieve League

595

Atharaght

One Man's Pass

Loch
Croleavy

Shanbally

Eagle's Nest

323

308

Scregeighter

START / FINISH

P **Bunglass**

a
n

to Carrick

an's

Shanbally

Scregeighter

Bunglass

8km

Carrigan Head

Looking towards Bunglass from the summit of Slieve League.

The path now moves away from the cliffs and crosses a couple of small rises. Climb diagonally across the heather-covered slopes of Crockrawer to reach a ridge with fine views at 435m. At one point the ridge narrows to an exposed rib of rock, half a metre wide, with dangerous drops on both sides. Although the OSi map marks One Man's Pass higher up the mountain, many Irish walkers believe the label has been misplaced, and this section is certainly more deserving of the name. In dry, calm conditions it is a straightforward scramble, but the exposure on the seaward side is awesome, so you will need to have a good head for heights. If the challenge doesn't appeal to you, take the easy alternative path on the right, which avoids all the difficulties and rejoins the crest of the ridge a little higher up.

The ridge broadens now and you emerge onto Slieve League's peat-covered eastern summit (560m). This is not the true summit, which is still a kilometre further on, but it is only 45m lower and for many walkers it is good enough. The views are similar from both points, and are predictably impressive. On a clear day it is possible to identify landmarks in several counties, including Croagh Patrick on the southern side of Donegal Bay. Closer to hand, look down the eastern slopes of Slieve League to spot the ruins of an old stone chapel and several beehive huts. These are the remnants of an Early Christian monastery, and serve as a reminder that this mountain has been considered sacred by Christian pilgrims for well over a thousand years.

The true summit lies north-west across another fine ridge (this is the section that has been wrongly marked on the map as One Man's Pass). This ridge is enjoyably airy, but can be crossed without breaking stride, and is much less daunting than the scramble lower down the mountain. Again, an alternative path on the right avoids all the exposure.

A trig pillar marks the official highpoint at 595m, and there are more fabulous views in all directions. When you have enjoyed the panorama sufficiently, simply reverse your outward route back to Bunglass below.

Traverse from Bunglass to Malin Beg

To complete the full traverse of Slieve League, continue to head west from the summit. Join a stony path that winds down onto the mountain's superb western shoulder. The descent is steep but you are rewarded by wonderful views south-east across the cliffs, which are punctuated by precarious pillars of shattered rock. As you reach the bottom of the slope, keep to the cliff edge for more dizzying views of the apparently overhanging precipice.

Descend across a stream, then climb again to cross two spurs that extend down from the moorland dome of Leahan. There is no longer a clear path underfoot, but continue to follow the cliff edge past several small streams, then swing north-west to reach the end of a rough track. This track leads around the bay, with the fine, horseshoe-shaped beach of Trabane immediately ahead. You can either descend steep grassy slopes directly onto the sand, or continue along the track to reach the car park at the top of the cove.

The 595m summit of Slieve League provides unrivalled coastal views.

ROUTE 8

Benwee Head

Grade:	4
Time:	4–5 hours
Distance:	12km (7½ miles)
Ascent:	480m (1,570ft)
Map:	OSi 1:50,000 sheets 22 and 23

A remote and spectacular walk along an undulating cliff line, past islands, sea stacks and a 250m-high coastal precipice in County Mayo.

Start & Finish: The route starts and finishes beside the post office in the centre of Carrowteige village, at a car park marked by a walk information board (grid reference: F821420). This is a Gaeltacht region so Carrowteige is signed as An Ceathrú Taidhg. Follow signs north off the R314 from Glenamoy (Gleann na Muaidhe). The village is around 21km north-east of Belmullet and 27km west of Ballycastle.

The north Mayo sea cliffs lie amid a remote and seldom-visited region, yet boast some of the most impressive coastal architecture in Ireland. The cliffs stretch for over 30km and reach up to 300m high. The precipice has been formed by thousands of years of Atlantic erosion, leaving vertical rock faces that are a literal cross section of the mountains

The bay just west of Doonvinalla is enclosed by a breathtaking arc of broken cliffs.

The sheer cliffs beneath Benwee Head reach up to 255m high.

above. Just offshore, countless sea stacks, islands and arches litter the base of the crags. Little wonder that Robert Lloyd Praeger, in his seminal guidebook *The Way That I Went*, called this 'the finest piece of cliff scenery in the country'.

The route begins with 3km along a country road, then diverts east across Benwee Head, where the cliffs reach 255m high. After 6km of fabulous, wild coastal walking, you follow a series of bog tracks back to the start.

Though it is not hard to follow, the route does involve 480m of ascent – equivalent to a moderate hillwalk – and is not signed for most of its distance. If you find this a daunting prospect, you might want to consider an easier alternative. There are two signed loop walks that also start and finish at the walk information board in Carrowteige, making lower coastal circuits to the west. The easiest of these is the 10km Children of Lir loop, which has 180m of ascent, takes 2½–3 hours to complete, and follows the blue arrows throughout. The scenery might not be as high or spectacular as Benwee Head, but the route is still very enjoyable, and offers a better option for less confident walkers.

As with all coastal routes, please exercise extreme caution near the cliff edge, and avoid walking in high winds or poor visibility.

The Walk

From the car park and walk information board, head west and climb gently along the main road. The first part of the route follows both the blue and

red waymarkers, walking counter to the official direction. The red arrows turn right after 1km, but you should continue straight ahead, still following the blue symbols. The road begins to descend now, and brings you to a T-junction after another kilometre. Turn right here and follow a narrow lane north towards the coast.

You arrive at the coast beside a metal and stone sculpture that commemorates the legend of the Children of Lir. This story tells of four children who were transformed into swans by their jealous stepmother. They were condemned to 900 years living on remote Irish waters, the final 300 of which were spent off this coast. When they finally reclaimed

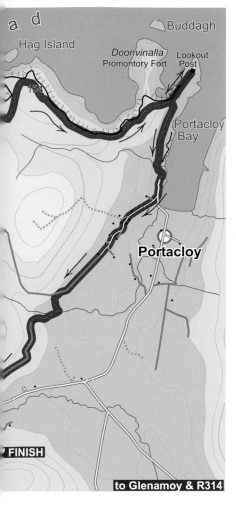

their human form on Inisglora, just west of Belmullet, they were so old they died and were buried there. The sculpture is perched at the very edge of a precipice, and there is an immediately striking view across the 100m-high cliffs that surround the inlet below.

Turn right at the sculpture and climb steeply east, again following the red markers. The signs soon veer inland along the banks of a stream called An Fiodan Dubh (The Black Ditch). This is where you leave the markers behind. Cross the stream and continue to follow the cliff line north-east across open, grassy ground. Increasingly expansive views west over Kid Island distract you from the effort of the climb.

Skirt a couple of tiny lochans perched right on the cliff edge before reaching the 255m summit of Benwee Head. As well as the dizzying drop beneath your feet, the fabulous panorama now includes the Stags of Broadhaven, Slieve League and Achill Island. Inland the shapely domes and ridges of the Nephin Beg range rear up beyond 30km of blanket bog.

Cross a fence as you start to descend, then continue north-east along the cliff line. Numerous islets lie just offshore here, with the towering stack of Hag Island prominent amongst them. Thousands of seabirds nest along these cliffs during the summer, but be careful near the edge as some sections are undercut.

Descend around a dramatic bay that is enclosed by a breathtaking arc of broken cliffs. At the north-eastern end of the bay, the headland of Doonvinalla lies at the end of a precipitous knife-edge ridge, which is undercut at the base by large sea caves. The headland once held an Iron Age promontory fort, but is surely in the process of becoming detached from the mainland.

The next headland is more stable, and you can walk out towards the end of the promontory to see the remains of an old lookout post and the word EIRE written in stones on the ground. Both landmarks are relics of the Second World War.

The hamlet of Portacloy can now be seen to the south, at the back of a long, narrow bay. Descend towards the houses, crossing a stream and passing through a gate to reach the pier. Despite tracing the coastline for the past 6km, this is your first opportunity to reach the water's edge. There is a fine, sandy beach just east of the pier if you want a longer break.

From the pier, follow the road south for 200m to a junction. Turn right here, then keep left at the next fork. This lane heads south-west and soon turns into a track. Follow the track as it sweeps west and begins to climb, then look out for a gap in the bank on the left. The gap arrives around 1km after the fork, and is marked by an old waymarking post. Turn left here and make your way across 300m of open moorland before joining another bog track.

Follow this track south-west across the hillside to a house, where the surface becomes paved underfoot. Continue along the lane to reach a junction with the main road. Turn right here and complete the final 250m up the hill and back to the start of the circuit.

Evening light over the cliffs of Benwee Head.

ROUTE 9
Erris Head

Grade:	2
Time:	1½–2 hours
Distance:	5km (3 miles)
Ascent:	100m (330ft)
Map:	OSi 1:50,000 sheet 22

A short but magnificent walk around the tip of this wild and remote headland in County Mayo.

Start & Finish: The route starts and finishes at Danish Cellar, at the northern tip of the Belmullet Peninsula (grid reference: F705397). From the roundabout in the centre of Belmullet town, head north along the R313. Roughly 600m later, continue straight ahead at a junction, following a brown sign for the 'Trailhead'. Continue to follow signs for the 'Trailhead' and 'Ceann Iorrais' (Erris Head in Irish), passing through several more junctions. After 8km you arrive at the end of the road, where a car park is set above the slipway at Danish Cellar. There is parking space here for around sixteen vehicles, and a map board marking the start of the route.

Erris Head is a name synonymous with gale warnings on the shipping forecast, a remote and exposed headland at the furthest reaches of Ireland's north-west coast. Head west from here and you'll land in Labrador, Canada; journey north and the first land you'll meet is the Arctic.

Walker beside the narrow chasm that separates Illandavuck from Erris Head.

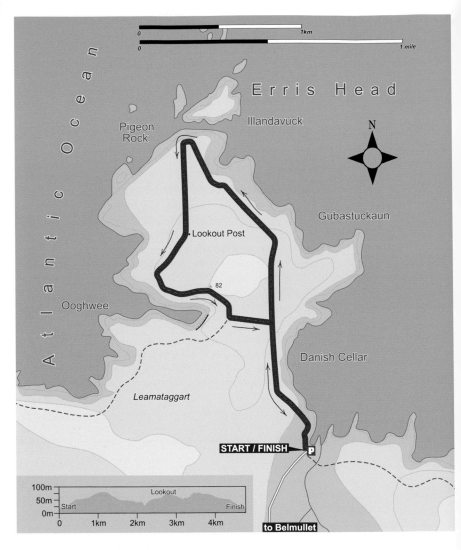

It is no surprise then that the coastline here is wild and spectacular. Fortunately, it is accessible too, thanks to a national looped walk that makes a circuit around the tip of the peninsula. The route is signed throughout and is short enough to suit families, though care is required in several places if you approach the edge of the cliffs. You will need decent boots too, because the terrain can be rough and wet underfoot.

The entire region around Erris Head has been designated a Special Area of Conservation. This is designed to protect the alpine heath on top of the headland, which provides a habitat for choughs and hares, as well as the cliffs at its fringes, where numerous species of seabird make their nests. If you can tear your eyes away from the filigreed coastline it is worth looking out for sea mammals too. Seals can often be seen swimming close to the shore, and numerous whale and dolphin sightings have been recorded.

The Walk

The route is signed throughout by purple arrows on black posts. Begin by crossing a metal stile beside the map board in the car park. This takes you into a grass field, where sheep often graze. Turn right and follow the fence around the edge of the field. Already there is a great view east, across Broadhaven Bay to the cliffs of Benwee Head. The cluster of jagged sea stacks just north of the mainland are the Stags of Broadhaven, five offshore pinnacles that rise almost 100m high, forming a distinctive landmark visible all along the north Mayo coast.

The route follows a raised bank of earth, which once acted as a boundary line between neighbouring parishes. Pass over two more stiles, then emerge onto open moorland. Follow the peaty path straight ahead, crossing several small bridges and negotiating occasional muddy patches.

After a gentle climb you will notice a line of marker posts coming across from the left; the route will return along here at the end of the circuit. Keep straight ahead for now, and climb across the promontory known as Gubastuckaun, or 'Beak of the Headland'. This is open terrain, however, so if you prefer to divert to the right and follow the coast around the edge of this promontory, there is nothing to stop you making your own route across the tussocks.

The official path soon becomes firmer underfoot, and dissipates altogether as you make the gentle descent towards the tip of Erris Head. The final waymarking post is set well back from the northern edge of the headland, but it is well worth exploring further and making your way (carefully!) to the edge of the cliff ahead. Here a sheer precipice 40m high drops abruptly into a narrow chasm, with the island of Illandavuck rearing steeply on the opposite side. This island was once attached to the mainland, but has been torn asunder by the mighty force of the Atlantic. Erris Head is an exposed spot beset by swirling ocean currents, and even in moderate swells it is easy to imagine the power of winter storms that cause such geological upheavals.

The route turns sharp left at Erris Head and begins to climb south, heading towards a prominent watchtower on top of the hill ahead. The building is the ruin of a concrete lookout post that dates from the Second World War. The post was manned continuously for five years, and the logbook reports frequent sightings of warships and US aircraft heading towards Northern Ireland. Today the views are more benign, with nothing but fabulous coastal scenery in every direction. To the south-east, at the back of Broadhaven Bay, you should also be able to spot the tower of Ballyglass Lighthouse, with the domes and ridges of the Nephin Beg Mountains providing a striking backdrop beyond.

As you begin the descent south-west from the lookout post, look out on the right for the word EIRE written on the ground in stones. This is another relic of the Second World War, designed to alert pilots to the fact that they were crossing neutral Ireland. Ahead, the lighthouse on Eagle Island is visible beyond a jumble of inshore sea stacks. The lighthouse dates from 1835, and the top of the tower sits 67m above the water. The island is located close to the continental shelf, however, and is frequently buffeted by huge waves, with spray clearing the top of the light on an annual basis.

The descent brings you to the edge of a deep coastal inlet known as Ooghwee, or 'Yellow Hole'. Turn left here and follow the rim of the chasm inland, then make a final short climb to the concrete trig pillar at the 82m summit of Erris Head. This is another fabulous vantage point, offering a 360° panorama that encompasses much of north-west Mayo.

The marker posts now lead east across a narrow neck of land and rejoin the outward route. Turn right at the trail junction, then retrace your initial steps back to the start.

Returning along the western side of Erris Head.

Achill Head & Croaghaun

Grade:	5
Time:	5–6 hours
Distance:	13km (8 miles)
Ascent:	920m (3,020ft)
Map:	OSi 1:50,000 sheet 30

A classic route over a truly spectacular Atlantic summit, above some of the highest sea cliffs in Europe.

Start & Finish: The route starts and finishes at the large, lower car park above Keem Strand (grid reference: F560042). Keem Strand is located at the end of the R319, some 8km west of Keel on Achill, County Mayo.

The great debate rages on: just where are Ireland's highest sea cliffs? Two coastal communities claim the bragging rights: Donegal's Slieve League awards itself the accolade, yet mighty Croaghaun on the western tip of Achill Island boasts cliffs that are both higher and marginally steeper. Yet the controversy misses the point: in terms of coastal walks, both Slieve League *and* Croaghaun are unsurpassed for grandeur.

On Croaghaun, the restless Atlantic has chiselled away enough rock to create a 2km stretch of cliffs that reaches over

The view towards Achill Head from the summit of Croaghaun.

550m high. The classic walking route around this epic landscape starts and finishes at Keem Strand, a remote and atmospheric cove that is one of the Signature Discovery Points of the Wild Atlantic Way. The sandy beach and sheltered waters here have long been popular with summer holidaymakers, and on a warm day there's nothing better than descending from Croaghaun's steep flanks to dive straight into the turquoise water below.

With 920m of ascent, this route has all the character of a full Irish hillwalk, and you should carry the local OSi map for extra safety. Indeed it is one of the country's classic mountain routes, boasting exposed ridges,

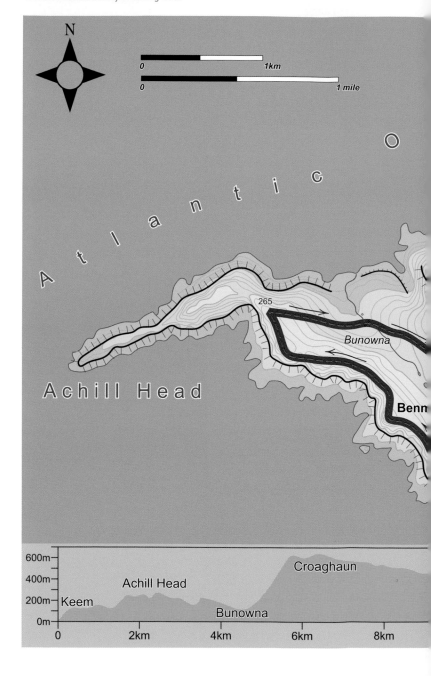

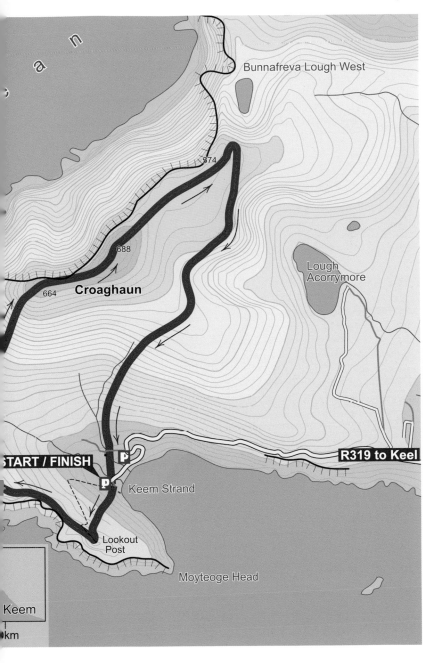

Bunnafreva Lough West

574

688

Croaghaun

664

Lough
Acorrymore

START / FINISH

P

P

Keem Strand

R319 to Keel

Lookout
Post

Moyteoge Head

Keem

km

Beautiful Keem Strand is one of the Signature Discovery Points of the Wild Atlantic Way.

stunning views and a 688m-high summit. If you're the sort of walker who prefers shorter outings, consider completing just the first part of the route, from Moyteoge Head, along the ridge to Achill Head. This trip gives a very good impression of the wild and dramatic coastline that forms the focal point of the longer route, without the big haul up to Croaghaun itself.

Whatever route you choose, be sure to check both the forecast and local weather conditions before you set out. Croaghaun's precipitous slopes often cause oceanic winds to rise so abruptly they form a persistent cap of cloud over the summit. It is worth waiting for clear, calm conditions to complete the walk, both so you can enjoy the fantastic views, and to avoid the inherent danger of walking above sheer cliffs in poor visibility or strong wind.

A natural jewel: Keem Strand seen from high on the slopes of Croaghaun.

The Walk

The first obvious goal from Keem Strand is the lookout post that lies atop Moyteoge Head to the south. From the southern end of the lower car park, follow a steep, informal trail that climbs to join the ridge just north-west of this landmark. The building itself was manned during both world

From Croaghaun, the view inland over Achill Island is also fantastic.

wars, and was also used in the 1950s and 1960s during the operation of the Achill Basking Shark Fishery. The basking sharks – the world's second biggest fish – were targeted for the oil in their liver, and spotters stationed at Moyteoge Head had the job of identifying them in the waters below. The Achill fishery recorded the greatest catch numbers in the world, with some 9,000 sharks caught here in just fourteen years. Unfortunately, the population crashed soon afterwards, and the species is now considered endangered in the north-east Atlantic.

After visiting the tower, continue north-west, climbing steadily along the cliff edge. You pass several small summits along the ridge, the finest of which is at 332m and affords dizzying views out to Achill Head. Continue all the way to the base of Achill Head, where you are rewarded by a stunning profile of Croaghaun's western cliffs. The adventurous may want to add a side trip along the promontory of Achill Head itself; the very tip is accessible with some modest scrambling, but the extreme exposure restricts the outing to those with nerves of steel.

The route then descends east, dropping into a small river valley that contains the remains of the old booley settlement of Bunowna. Here, as many as sixteen oval-shaped huts used to serve as summer dwellings for shepherds while livestock were grazed and milked on the mountain nearby. Beyond Bunowna, the steep western flank of Croaghaun must now be tackled head on. By traversing further south-east you gain slightly easier ground, but there is no avoiding the gradient in the last half of the climb, as you weave through large blocks and outcrops of rock to reach Croaghaun's western top at 664m.

The peak is located right at the edge of the cliffs, and you are greeted by a sudden, gut-wrenching view down vertiginous slopes that drop all the way to the Atlantic. To the north-east, a further 4km of dramatic cliffs stretch away to Saddle Head. Once you have recovered from the initial shock, you can also appreciate the wider 360° panorama, which encompasses much of the coastline of west Mayo. The mountain of Croagh Patrick is easily identifiable, as are the offshore islands of Clare Island and Inishturk.

Now follow the cliff line east, descending briefly across a small saddle before climbing again towards the main summit of Croaghaun. The ridge is pleasantly exposed on both sides, with steep slopes sweeping away towards Keem Strand to the south. The top is marked by a small cairn, and a continuation of the fabulous views.

Beyond the main summit the southern slopes become gentler but the drama to the north continues. Descend north-east, continuing along the cliff edge towards an obvious promontory. On the way you pass a section where a massive chunk of the cliff is in the process of parting company with the rest of the mountain, and it is humbling to imagine the impact below when this eventually happens.

The promontory provides a good perspective back across the summit of Croaghaun, and affords new views north-east across the deep corrie holding beautiful Bunnafreva Lough West. Several other fine lakes are also visible further north-east, including Ireland's lowest corrie lake, just above Annagh Strand. These remote loughs are all inaccessible except by foot and must have been visited by very few people, and it feels like a privilege to gaze across such a secret corner of Ireland.

Turn south at the promontory and descend gradually to the rim of the corrie holding Lough Acorrymore. The adjacent water treatment works means this lake provides water for the whole of Achill Island. Pass around the top of the corrie, then continue south-west across the broad eastern spur of Croaghaun.

From the top of this shoulder, Keem Strand and the old coastguard station behind it become visible below. It seems a simple task to drop down to the cove, but thick heather on the intervening slope makes progress more awkward than it should be. Head for a strip of grass along the eastern edge of a small stream, which provides the easiest line of descent. It is now just a short hop back to the car park where the route began.

Four kilometres of cliffs separate Saddle Head from Croaghaun.

Minaun Heights

Grade:	4
Time:	4–5 hours
Distance:	13km (8 miles)
Ascent:	540m (1,770ft)
Map:	OSi 1:50,000 sheet 30

This impressive trip takes you past a long stretch of magnificent cliff line, with fabulous views throughout.

Start & Finish: The circuit starts and finishes at a car park above Camport Bay in Dooega village (grid reference: L675986), on Achill, County Mayo. To reach Dooega, follow the R319 over Achill Sound towards Keel. Around 4km west of Achill Sound, turn left, following signs to Dooega (Dumha Eige). Turn left at the T-junction at the end of the road, and the car park is 300m later on the right.

If you have two vehicles, you can also start at the summit car park at the top of Minaun Heights (grid reference: F670028). To get there, turn left off the R319 5km west of Achill Sound, following the northernmost road to Dooega. Around 2km later, turn right up a steep lane signed to Minaun Heights.

The view over Dooega Head and Clare Island from Minaun Heights.

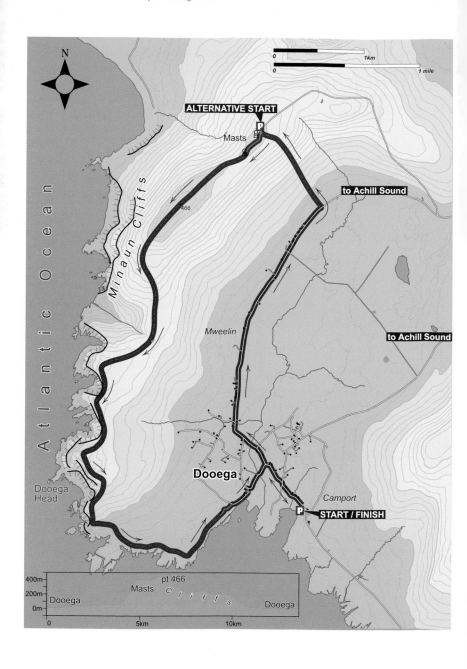

The route starts and finishes in the coastal village of Dooega.

I n terms of coastal scenery, Achill Island is a walker's paradise. The most famous sea cliffs lie beneath Croaghaun, on the western tip of the island. But these are not the only cliffs on Achill – far from it. Though not as high as Croaghaun, the Minaun Heights are equally as impressive and far more accessible, and provide a wonderful viewpoint across the entire island.

There are two ways to complete this route. If you have two vehicles you can start at the summit car park and follow the cliffs downhill to Dooega, enjoying the rare pleasure of a route with 540m of descent but just 135m of ascent. Allow 3½ hours for this 9km route. With one vehicle you will have to factor in an extra climb of 400m, and should complete the full circuit as described below.

The route is not signed, but navigation is relatively straightforward. The full circuit starts with 4km of road walking, then switches to open hillside and grassy clifftop. Much of the route is spent in close proximity to a sheer drop, so it is best to avoid walking in poor visibility or high winds. Note too that the Minaun Heights are spelled Menawn on the OSi map.

The Walk

From Camport Bay car park, turn left onto the road. Continue straight ahead across three road junctions in Dooega village, then begin to follow a minor road north beneath Minaun Heights. Continue along the road for around 3.5km, until you have passed the final house. The fence on the left stops just past this building. Turn west here and begin to climb directly up the steep, heather-covered slope, aiming for the communication masts that mark Minaun's eastern summit.

A sustained ascent of 340 vertical metres brings you to the top, where you will find a large parking area. The view here is immediately impressive,

The coastal scenery along the Minaun Heights is spectacular throughout.

and a good reward for the effort of the climb. Directly beneath you the 4km-long beach of Trawmore sweeps west towards Croaghaun, and much of northern Achill can also be seen.

Turn south-west at the car park and follow a stone track past the left side of a fenced building. The track weaves past various communication masts before coming to an end. Continue straight ahead over the peaty ground, climbing towards the prominent cairn and statue that mark the 466m summit. The statue of the Virgin Mary was donated to the islanders by an American woman of Irish descent, and was placed on this high point as a blessing to all those living beneath it.

Continue south-west from the summit, passing a series of small, modern cairns. Descend across broad slopes for 800m, then swing east around an inlet to a col. A series of quartzite cairns offers guidance across these lower slopes, some of which are old funeral stones. These are a legacy from the days when Kildavnet Church, on the south-eastern tip of Achill, held the only graveyard on the island. Funeral processions from villages in the north-west would pass over Minaun on their way to the cemetery, and the cairns mark the spots where coffins were laid while the pallbearers took a rest.

Veer south-west at the col and climb a heather-covered slope to the top of the next rise, where you are rewarded with the first fantastic view north along the cliffs themselves. In some places the rock is plumb vertical, dropping 250m to the sea below. The furthest cliffs, situated at the eastern end of Trawmore, are known as Cathedral Rocks, and harbour a series of caves that can be visited from the beach at low tide.

Now you have joined the cliff line proper, it is essentially a case of tracing the edge of the cliffs around the western and southern reaches of Dooega Head. The terrain underfoot is a mixture of short heather and cropped grass, and a faint path is visible for most of the way.

The coastal scenery becomes more and more spectacular as you progress. First you round a series of small inlets where the rock drops 250m to the ocean. Then, as you near the tip of the headland, the focus suddenly switches to the south. Beyond a rocky promontory, the lighthouse and cliffs of Clare Island come into view some 12km out to sea, backed by the myriad peaks of Connemara and south Mayo.

The cliffs begin to lose height now and a relatively steep, heathery descent brings you down almost to sea level. Aim for an old stone wall that runs along the top of the shoreline, following this past several small fissures and rock arches that have been sculpted by the power of the waves.

The OSi map indicates two promontory forts around Dooega Head. Though there is no obvious sign of these today, archaeologists have identified them as part of a chain of forts that once circled Achill's coastline. Together the sites provide evidence of the thriving communities that lived on the island during the Iron Age.

Continue around the south-eastern corner of the headland, passing between the wall and the shore. At times you may be forced onto the rocks themselves to avoid the occasional boggy patch. As you turn north-east towards Dooega a rough track begins to consolidate underfoot. Follow the track to a junction with a tarmac lane, and continue straight ahead along the road. Keep straight ahead at the first road junction and turn right at the second, then walk the final 800m back to the car park.

Descending towards Dooega Head near the end of the route.

ROUTE 12
Clare Island

Grade:	4
Time:	5–6 hours
Distance:	15km (9½ miles)
Ascent:	600m (1,970ft)
Map:	OSi 1:50,000 sheet 30

Tremendous views, impressive sea cliffs and a 462m summit are all features of Ireland's most mountainous island.

Start & Finish: The route starts and finishes at Clare Island pier (grid reference: L715852), County Mayo.

Clare Island Ferries (Tel: 098 23737; www.clareislandferry.com) and **O'Malley Ferries** (Tel: 086 8870 814; www.omalleyferries.com) both operate between Clare Island and Roonagh Quay on the mainland. The crossing costs €15 return, and takes around 20 minutes. Both companies offer daily sailings all year round, and frequent services mean it is quite possible to fit the route into a day trip. Contact the operators for full schedule information.

Roonagh Quay is situated around 28km west of Westport, via the R335 through Lousiburgh.

Standing guard at the mouth of Clew Bay, Clare Island is a rugged, cliff-fringed outpost that extends to ten square kilometres. Dominated by Knockmore (462m), it is the most mountainous of all the islands of Ireland, and boasts the sort of walking that is normally associated with hilly regions on the mainland. Here, however, the combination of height and island location means that walkers are rewarded by coastal views from a unique perspective. Add several kilometres of impressive vertical sea cliffs and throw in a little island atmosphere, and you have a truly tremendous Atlantic outpost to explore.

The harbour in Fawnglass where the ferry arrives.

The sea cliffs reach 400m high on Clare Island's north-west coast.

To get the best from the island, you really need to gain a perspective over the north-west coast. Here, beneath the summit of Knockmore, sheer cliffs drop some 400m to the waves below. The route described here makes the most of this dramatic scenery, and also allows you to complete a full circumnavigation of the island.

The mountain ascent is the centrepiece of the circuit, sandwiched between 4km of quiet laneways at the start and 5km of tarmac to finish. Vehicles are few and far between on islands such as this, however, and constant coastal views mean the road sections are no great chore.

Note that the section along the north coast follows precipitous cliffs, and should be avoided in poor visibility and high winds.

The Walk

From the ferry pier in Fawnglass, walk around the harbour and pass a tower house that once served as a castle for Grace O'Malley. O'Malley (1530–1603) – or Granuaile as she is also known – is the island's most celebrated daughter. An infamous pirate queen, she once controlled much of Connacht, and was a constant thorn in the side of the English and their allies as she plundered their ships in Clew Bay.

Turn right at the first junction and follow a small road around the back of the beach, which is a focal point of activity during the summer. Keep left at another junction in front of the community centre, following signs for the lighthouse. The lane passes through several gateways with adjacent stiles as it climbs across a modest spur, then winds across two further rises.

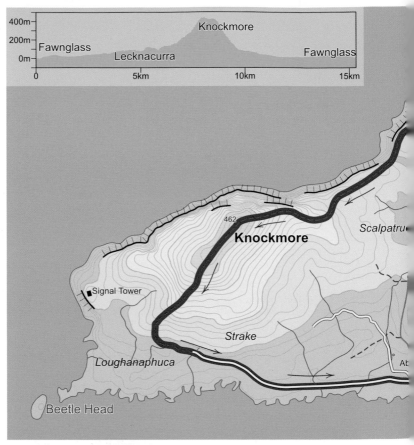

Passing a clifftop pool, with Knockmore rising behind.

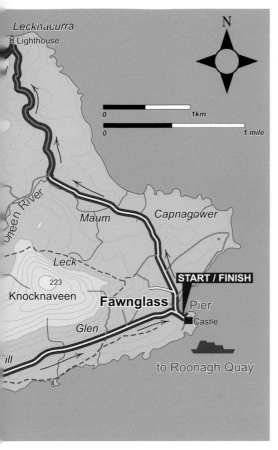

Around 2km from Fawnglass, the road comes to another junction. Turn right here and begin a steady climb that continues all the way to the northern tip of the island. The road dwindles to a single-lane track as you near the coast, and the scenery becomes progressively wilder. A final push brings you to the lighthouse, which dates from 1806 and is the only double-towered lighthouse in Ireland. The light was decommissioned in 1965 because its location, perched on the cliff edge some 100m above the water, meant it was often shrouded in mist. Today it operates as a private guesthouse.

This is a good vantage point from which to appreciate the sheer cliffs that stretch away to the west. From the lighthouse, head south-west across open ground and begin to follow the cliff edge, staying on the landward side of a fence. Cropped grass and firm turf ease your passage over a series of short but steep undulations, with the fine views over the sea cliffs and Knockmore providing constant distraction.

The route swings west as you progress onto the east ridge of Knockmore and begin the unrelenting climb to the top. Rougher terrain and tussocks take over underfoot as you gain height, and you may need to veer inland slightly over the steepest sections. Fortunately, the views from the summit trig pillar more than justify the effort of the ascent; the panorama includes the islands of Inishturk and Inishbofin to the south, as well as the mountains of Connemara, Mayo and Achill Island.

From the summit, head south-west across the broad, peaty summit ridge, passing a large stone cairn on the way. Now descend steeply from the edge of the plateau, following a shoulder south-west towards the road

The route follows the cliff edge south-west from Clare Island Lighthouse.

and bungalows below. As you descend, the ruins of a Napoleonic signal tower can be seen near the north-western tip of the island. This provides an easy detour for those with the energy – a track then leads from the tower to the end of the road.

Back on the main circuit, join the road and turn left. This road leads all the way back to Fawnglass, some 5.5km away. After 3km you come to a road junction, where there is an option of a short detour to visit the island's Cistercian abbey. If you want to do this, turn left, then take the right 150m later. Cistercian monks first arrived here during the thirteenth century AD. Amongst other treasures the abbey contains some of the best preserved medieval wall and ceiling paintings in Ireland, and a canopy tomb that is believed to be the burial place of Grace O'Malley. To view the inside of the building, collect a key from the adjacent house.

When you have finished exploring the site, turn left out of the church grounds, then take the first right and return to the main road. It is now a simple matter of following this road back to the pier where you started.

Croagh Patrick

Out-and-back from Murrisk		Out-and-back via Ben Goram	
Grade:	4	**Grade:**	4
Time:	3½–4½ hours	**Time:**	3½–4½ hours
Distance:	7km (4½ miles)	**Distance:**	8km (5 miles)
Ascent:	750m (2,460ft)	**Ascent:**	700m (2,300ft)
Map:	The route straddles three OSi 1:50,000 sheets – numbers 30, 31 and 37.	**Map:**	The route straddles two OSi 1:50,000 sheets – numbers 30 and 37.

A choice of two routes climb to fabulous coastal views at the summit of Ireland's holy mountain.

The quartzite pyramid of Croagh Patrick in County Mayo is perhaps the most famous, and definitely the most popular mountain in Ireland. It attracts around a million walkers annually, some 25,000 of whom congregate on Reek Sunday, the traditional day of religious pilgrimage on the last Sunday in July.

The mountain's attractions are twofold. First, there's the history: the summit holds the remains of a prehistoric settlement dating from 300 BC, and was an important site of pagan celebration. Some 700 years later St Patrick climbed to the top, where he fasted for forty days and forty nights. Since then Croagh Patrick has become a place of Christian pilgrimage, and has been embraced as Ireland's holy mountain. Mass is still said in the summit church, the current version of which dates from 1905 and is the highest church in Ireland.

Besides its religious symbolism, the 764m summit makes a superlative viewpoint. Its location on southern shore of Clew Bay ensures a wide-reaching coastal panorama stretching from Inishturk to Clare Island and Achill. Beneath the peak to the north, myriad islands lie scattered across Clew Bay. The islets are submerged glacial drumlins, and are so numerous they are said to number one for every day of the year.

The most popular way to climb Croagh Patrick is via the tourist path from Murrisk. This route starts at a large, serviced car park. The trail is extremely well trodden and obvious throughout, and you will have the security of other walkers around you. However, the path's breadth and popularity often leads hillwalkers who prefer more natural surrounds to look for an alternative approach. For confident and independent walkers, the route via Ben Goram offers a much quieter, more satisfying experience,

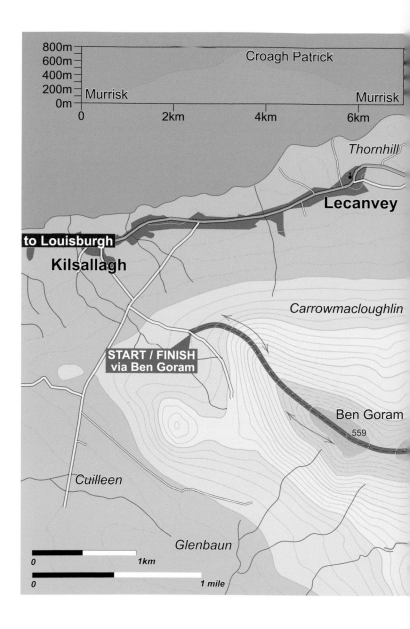

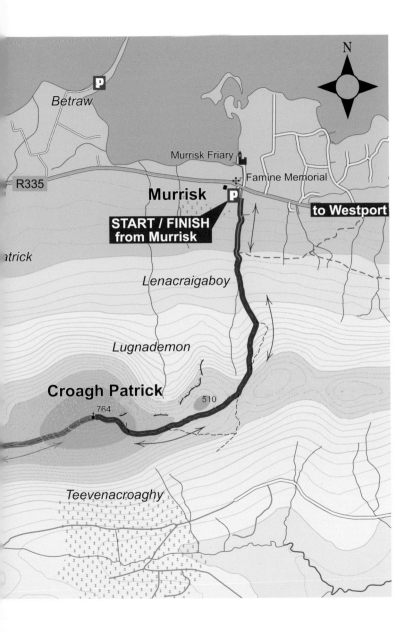

Family celebrations at Croagh Patrick's rocky summit.

far from the maddening crowds that gather at Murrisk. Of course if you have two vehicles, it is also possible to combine both routes and make a full traverse of the mountain.

It is important to understand, however, that there is no easy way up Croagh Patrick. The summit slopes are unrelentingly steep, and covered with loose rocks that threaten to dislodge with every step. The large number of inexperienced and unprepared walkers means incidents are common, and the local mountain rescue team averages over thirty operations here each year. Take all the normal precautions associated with climbing a 760m mountain, including wearing good boots and carrying plenty of food and warm and waterproof clothing.

Out-and-back from Murrisk

Start & Finish: This route starts and finishes at a large car park at the bottom of the tourist path in Murrisk (grid reference: L919823). There is a €3 charge for parking here all day, but facilities include toilets and a visitor centre offering a restaurant, craft shop, hot showers and secure lockers. Murrisk is located 8km west of Westport along the R335 to Louisburgh.

The Walk

The route begins from the south-eastern corner of the car park, where there are various stalls selling snacks and walking sticks. Follow a gravel footpath to a lane, then turn right. Pass the visitor centre and climb along the tarmac for 300m. At the end of the road, continue up a flight of wide steps to reach a white statue of Saint Patrick, with fine, open views to the mountain ahead.

The statue marks the end of the constructed surface. Continue ahead onto an obvious earthen trail studded with stones and rocks. On a good day the route is clearly visible, climbing south towards a col at the eastern side of Croagh Patrick. The ascent starts immediately, and continues steadily until you reach the col, some 450 vertical metres above.

The path swings right (west) at the col, and the angle of the slope relents enough to allow you to gather your breath. There is a toilet block here, and the mountain's first pilgrim station, with a plaque prescribing an impressive list of rituals to be performed by the devout.

The stony trail is now as wide as a country lane. It contours along the southern side of the ridge for 400m, bringing you inexorably closer to the huge, intimidating rock cone that protects the mountain's summit. The bad news is that the climb is every bit as steep as it looks. Steel yourself for an unrelenting ascent of 300 vertical metres, with loose rocks and scree causing inadvertent downward slides and necessitating the use of hands in places. Depending on the time of year the route may also be busy with people, and you should watch out for rocks being dislodged from above.

Between thirty and forty-five minutes of uphill grind should bring you to the top. The summit of Croagh Patrick is an unusual place in terms of Irish mountains. On one hand, it is the country's most urbanised top, cluttered with buildings and shelters, including another toilet block and a second pilgrim station. On the other, there is no denying the natural splendour of the view, and you will probably want to linger a while to take it all in.

When you're ready, return to the car park by reversing your outward route. Take extra care on the descent between the summit and col, because loose rock can be even more treacherous going down.

Out-and-back via Ben Goram

Start & Finish: This route starts and finishes along a minor road west of Croagh Patrick at grid reference L874808. From Murrisk, continue west along the R335 to the village of Leckanvey. Around 1.5km west of Leckanvey, turn left onto a road signed for Chris Harper Artist Art Studio. Follow this road for 1km, then turn left. Park beside a gate on the right around 700m further on.

The Walk

Begin by hopping over a wire fence on the eastern side of the road and heading towards the base of Ben Goram's north-west ridge. When you reach the ridge, turn right and begin to climb along its apex. A footpath consolidates underfoot as you gain height, and there are increasingly expansive views over Clew Bay and the offshore islands of Mayo.

Dawn reflection of Croagh Patrick in the waters of Clew Bay.

Follow the path along the top of the ridge, with precipitous slopes to the west. Pass a prominent pillar-like cairn, with a mixture of peat and rock underfoot. The angle of ascent relents shortly before you reach the 559m summit of Ben Goram, which is marked by a small cairn.

Descend south-east to a peat col, then begin the final climb up the rocky pyramid of Croagh Patrick. Another trail soon joins the path from the left; this is the remnant of a miners' track, built in 1989 after small amounts of gold were found within the area's quartz veins. Local opposition to the desecration of Ireland's holy mountain meant the mining project was eventually abandoned.

Partway up the slope you pass three cairns marking Reilig Mhuire, or The Virgin's Cemetery. This is Croagh Patrick's third and final pilgrim station, and also a possible pre-Christian burial site. A final, steep ascent brings you up the rocks to the summit, where you will meet the crowds that have ascended via the tourist path. Take your time to enjoy the wonderful view, then descend back into peace and solitude by returning the way you came.

ROUTE 14

Inishturk

Grade:	3
Time:	3½–4½ hours
Distance:	10km (6 miles)
Ascent:	290m (950ft)
Map:	OSi 1:50,000 sheet 37

Explore a modest mountain summit and 130m-high sea cliffs on the circumnavigation of this charming Atlantic island.

Start & Finish: The route starts and finishes at Inishturk pier (grid reference: L620749). **O'Malley Ferries** (Tel: 098 25045; www.omalleyferries.com) have regular services to Inishturk from Roonagh Quay on the mainland. The crossing costs €20 return, and takes roughly forty minutes. There are daily sailings all year round, and departure times generally allow plenty of opportunity to fit the walk into a day trip. Contact the operator for full schedule information. Roonagh Quay is located around 28km west of Westport, via the R335 through Lousiburgh.

Inishturk is one of the most remote inhabited islands in Ireland, lying 10km off the shore of County Mayo. Yet in spite of its relative isolation, it never feels like a lonely outpost. Instead it finds the perfect balance between wild scenery and welcoming hospitality, with friendly inhabitants, a picturesque harbour, a modest mountain summit and 130m-high sea cliffs thrown in for good measure.

The scenery on Inishturk is impressive, and the high proportion of commonage means walkers can wander freely over much of the land. There are two signed loop walks on the island, and this route follows the marker posts at the beginning and end of its circuit. However, the signed routes bypass many of the island's finest natural features, so the route described here diverts across open ground for its central section, taking you across the summit of a 191m-high hill and along a 2km stretch of soaring cliff line. Navigation is not difficult here, but if you are daunted by the idea of unsigned terrain, stick to the purple arrows of the 8km Mountain Common Loop instead.

The off-road terrain consists of a mixture of cropped grass and exposed rock outcrops, providing a firm surface that is perfect for walking. The only proviso is that the western part of the route passes along exposed cliff tops, so care is needed near the edge. As always, avoid walking in poor visibility and high winds.

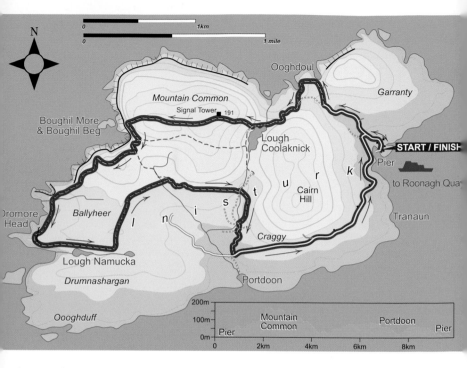

The Walk

From the ferry pier, walk to the harbour entrance, past the map board detailing the two signed walks on the island. This circuit follows the marked routes for the first 1.5km. Begin by joining the only real road on the island, and following it for 300m to a junction. Turn right here and head uphill along another lane for 500m. Now pass through a metal gate and join a rough stone track, which continues across the rock-studded commonage ahead.

Though you will return to the track shortly, it is worth starting with a detour north to the coast. Turn right just inside the gate and follow a wall to the top of an 80m-high chasm known as Ooghdoul. The sound and smell of seabirds herald your arrival at the sheer-sided inlet, and during the summer you should be able to spot nesting fulmars and their chicks on the cliffs below. It is an impressive introduction to the island's wild side.

Turn left at the chasm and follow the coastline south-west. There are great views across the bay to the hill known as Mountain Common, which is topped by the ruins of a prominent signal tower. This summit is your next goal, but the easiest way to reach it is via the stone track. Swing back south across rocky ground, then rejoin the track and turn right.

Looking towards the mainland from the east coast of Inishturk.

Climb gently along the track to Lough Coolaknick, which provides the island's only reliable source of fresh water. At the north-western tip of the lake, leave the signed walks and continue ahead across open ground. A steady ascent brings you to the top of Mountain Common, the highest point of the island at 191m. The summit is marked by a trig point and Napoleonic signal tower, as well as fine views across Achill Island, Clare Island and the mainland mountains of Connemara and Mayo.

From the summit, head west across a series of hummocks to reach the coast. Take care as you near the edge because the cliffs here are the highest on the island, dropping vertically for 130m to the waves below.

Several rock stacks decorate the base of the precipice, and two of them have names: Boughil More and Boughil Beg, which translate as 'Big Fella' and 'Little Fella' respectively. The pinnacles cause the ocean to surge and swirl below, and the sense of power and space is really quite exhilarating.

Turn left at the cliff edge and begin to follow the coastline south. You pass above several more chasms and viewpoints before the cliffs begin to lose height. Cross two pretty

Fishing boats in Inishturk harbour.

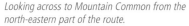
Looking across to Mountain Common from the north-eastern part of the route.

The rock stacks of Boughil More and Boughil Beg from Inishturk's western cliffs.

streams, then climb slightly to reach Dromore Head. This final promontory provides a fine view south to the island of Inishbofin.

Turn inland at Dromore Head and go east along the edge of an inlet. Pass Lough Namucka and continue east until you meet a stone wall. Turn left and follow the wall north for 600m to a corner. Turn right here, still following the wall. Soon you rejoin the walk signed with purple arrows; continue ahead in tandem with this route, heading east for another 700m to reach a gravel road.

You emerge beside the island's Gaelic football pitch, a wonderfully rugged playing field that has been squeezed onto one of the only flat spots on the island. Turn right onto the road and continue to a junction with the coast road 1km later.

The main route turns left here, but if you have time, it is worth making a 400m detour to visit the natural harbour of Portdoon. To do this, turn right onto the road, then left 100m later. The first human inhabitants arrived on Inishturk in 4000 BC, and most of the island's Neolithic remains are clustered around this inlet. Some 5,000 years later, a band of Viking pirates also landed here, and constructed the promontory fort marked on the map. The rocks surrounding the creek shielded their boats from passing vessels and provided an ideal hiding place from which to launch their raids.

When you're ready, return to the main road and turn right, following the tarmac around the south-eastern corner of the island. Another possible detour, this time to a sandy beach, comes near the top of the hill before the final descent to the pier. Pass through a metal gate on the right, following a sign for Tranaun. Descend across a field to reach a delightful cove, which provides a perfect place to cool off on a hot day. Alternatively, just 20m beyond the gate is the Community Centre, where refreshments are served from the bar.

Follow the road downhill for the final 800m to return to the pier.

ROUTE 15
Killary Harbour

Grade:	3
Time:	2–2½ hours
Distance:	6.5km (4 miles)
Ascent:	160m (520ft)
Map:	OSi 1:50,000 sheet 37, or Harvey Superwalker 1:30,000 *Connemara*.

This short circuit on the shore of Killary Harbour features a famine road, a deserted hamlet and wonderful mountain scenery.

Start & Finish: The route starts and finishes at Rosroe harbour (grid reference: L769650) in County Galway. To reach Rosroe, turn west off the N59 some 7km south-west of Leenane and 13km north-east of Letterfrack, following a sign for Tullycross. After 5km, veer right onto a minor road signed to Rosroe Pier. Continue for 3km to the end of the road. There is plenty of parking space beside the pier, but please be careful not to impede access to the slipway.

Set amidst stunning mountain scenery in northern Connemara, Killary Harbour is often described as Ireland's only true fjord. A long, narrow sea inlet that stretches inland for 16km, it reaches a maximum depth of 45m. The harbour was once a deep mountain valley carved by the glaciers of the last Ice Age. When the climate warmed up, sea levels rose and the valley was flooded, leaving a tidal firth surrounded on all sides by steep, craggy peaks.

Given the beauty of the region, it is no wonder that Killary Harbour has become a Signature Discovery Point of the Wild Atlantic Way. Yet this route offers more than just an exploration of the area's scenery; it is also a journey into its rather poignant past. The Great Famine of 1845–49 was felt particularly harshly in this part of the country, and evidence of the hardship of that period is impossible to avoid. A deserted village and a famine relief road are two of the main legacies of that era visited during the walk.

Crossing the stone stile at the western side of Foher.

91

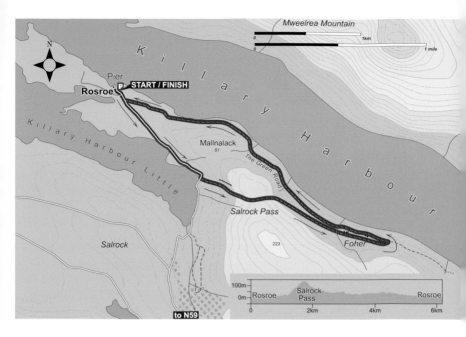

The circuit starts and finishes at the tiny hamlet of Rosroe, at the mouth of Killary Harbour. After 1km along a country lane, a rugged path takes you over Salrock Pass, the modest highpoint of the circuit at 130m. You descend to join a grassy track known locally as 'The Green Road', which takes you along the southern shore of Killary Harbour and back to the start. The route is not signed but navigation is relatively simple throughout. You will appreciate decent boots, however, because the terrain is rough in places and some sections may be muddy after rain.

The Walk

Rosroe harbour is a scenic and secluded place to start the walk. There are often colourful fishing boats tied up in the harbour, and the mountain rearing skyward just across Killary Harbour is Mweelrea, the highest peak in Connacht at 814m. Rosroe is also home to a salmon farming company, and you may well see their fish pens in the water just west of the quay.

From the pier, begin by walking south-east along the road you arrived on. After 200m you come to a grassy track on the left, located just before a whitewashed cottage. The end of the track is enclosed by stone walls, and marked by a sign saying 'No Dogs Allowed'. This is the end of the Green Road, the track you will return along at the end of the circuit.

Rosroe harbour, where the route starts and finishes.

Continue ahead along the road for now, undulating along the tarmac to the shore of Killary Harbour Little. Also known as Little Killary, this pretty Atlantic inlet mimics the shape of the larger fjord to the north. Around 1km from the start the road draws close to the water for a second time and makes a sharp right turn. At the apex of this bend, turn left and pass through a gap in a fence. A procession of power lines marches up the hillside here, and the route follows beneath the poles. The power lines may not be pretty, but they do provide useful navigational guidance.

Pass over a small stream and turn left up a faint track. Follow the track as it climbs steeply beneath a band of cliffs, decorated at the bottom with a jumble of blocks and boulders that have calved away from the precipice. After 600m you arrive at Salrock Pass. This is highest point of the route, and provides views of both Little Killary and Killary Harbour. According to legend, this pass was formed by the devil when he dragged the local Saint Roc over the hills with a chain. This is also an old smuggling route, used to transport illicit goods landed at Little Killary inland for further distribution.

The first part of the descent down the eastern side of the pass is steep, but it provides great views across to Mweelrea mountain. After 120m, where the power lines turn right, you arrive at a junction of a fence and stone wall on your right. Cross the wire fence at the corner, then turn immediately left through a metal pedestrian gate. Now turn right and follow a faint path alongside the wall, making a gradual, diagonal descent towards Killary Harbour.

You are now at the top of the deserted settlement of Foher, a hamlet that was depopulated around the time of the Great Famine. Some of the houses are roofless stone ruins, while others have been partially restored.

Winter reflections in Killary Harbour.

Old field boundaries and lazy beds (former potato drills) can also be seen scattered across the slope, providing an evocative memorial to the community that once lived here.

Drop onto a grass track at the eastern end of the hamlet. This is the Green Road, a famine relief project that was constructed in 1846 by starving locals in return for food rations. Turn left and begin to follow the track west, contouring above the shore of Killary Harbour. Out on the water lines of floats mark the fish cages and mussel rafts of the fjord's thriving aquaculture industry.

Pass along the base of Foher and climb over a stone stile in the wall to the west. The track now dwindles to a single-file path and climbs around a rock outcrop. At the side of the path, the retaining walls of the famine road can be seen clearly.

The landscape is now more rugged, dotted with boulders and bands of rock. It is not long, however, before the boats and buildings of Rosroe come into view ahead. Pass along the southern side of a high stone wall to reach the end of the track, beside the whitewashed cottage you passed at the start of the route. Rejoin the road and turn right to complete the final 200m back to Rosroe Pier.

Walking alongside the stone wall on the descent to Foher.

ROUTE 16

Omey Island

Grade:	3
Time:	2½–3 hours
Distance:	8km (5 miles)
Ascent:	110m (360ft)
Map:	OSi 1:50,000 sheet 37

Cross a tidal causeway to explore the long history and beautiful scenery of this unique island.

Start & Finish: The route starts and finishes at a car park just south of Claddaghduff Quay (grid reference: L578564). Most people approach the area via the N59. Turn west off the N59 around 3km north of Clifden, following a sign to Omey Island. Continue for 8km to the village of Claddaghduff, then turn left beside the church, again following a sign for Omey. Continue for 1km and park at the car park at the end of the road.

S ituated near the western tip of County Galway, Omey Island is a unique place to explore. Its low but varied shoreline and open machair provide easy walking, and there are fine views all around. But this is an island with a difference: it is only really an island for half the time. With every low tide, a sandy causeway is revealed, connecting Omey to the mainland. Time your visit right and you can skip across the sand, negating the need for a boat.

The northern shore of Omey Island consists of sandy beaches studded with rocks.

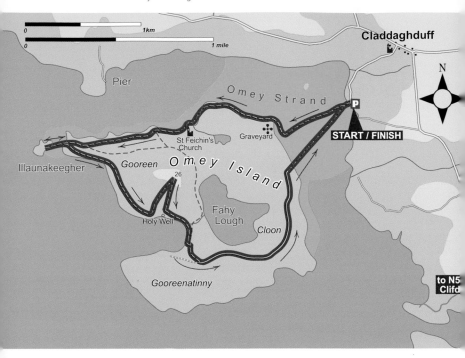

Besides the scenery, the most remarkable thing about Omey is its history. Though it now has just one permanent resident, the island supported a population of over 400 people until the 1840s. But even that is just the tip of the iceberg: recent coastal erosion has revealed human habitation stretching back for millennia.

Much of the activity centred around the island's northern shore. In 1992, a detailed archaeological excavation of this area revealed a multi-period site, whose earliest remains consisted of a prehistoric midden deposit. Then came several small structures and artefacts dating from the early Bronze Age. Above that lay a cemetery from late pagan or Early Christian times, followed by another burial pit established during the Middle Ages. The final layer

The medieval ruin of St Feichin's Church occupies the site of an earlier monastery.

View towards Cruagh Island from the cairn on the tidal islet of Illaunakeegher.

included the foundations of several houses built during the 1800s. This fascinating cross section of Irish history demonstrates that what may seem today like a remote coastal outpost often may have served as a thriving communal centre in times gone by.

One of the most interesting periods of Omey's history began in the seventh century, when St Feichin arrived on the island. The saint dedicated his life to establishing a series of monasteries along Ireland's western seaboard, including one here at Omey. His task was not always easy, however: records state that when he arrived here the local pagan population proved intractable, throwing Feichin's possessions into the sea. The islanders remained unswayed despite the miraculous restoration of these items, but finally succumbed to Christianity after Feichin demonstrated his powers by restoring two dead monks to life.

From a practical point of view, the main challenge of a trip to Omey is getting the tide right. The causeway is exposed from around mid-tide to mid-tide. To find daily tide times, use an online resource like www.easytide.com, and select the timetable for Clifden Bay. Try to leave the mainland around two or two and a half hours before low tide. Tide times are also displayed on an information board in the car park at the start, so you can double-check your calculations before heading out.

Even when the tide is out, Omey Strand remains rather wet in places. If you do not have a good pair of boots, consider going barefoot or wearing water sandals for the crossing.

The Walk

From the car park, begin by descending the slipway and dropping onto Omey Strand. A line of blue arrows marches south-west across the sand, marking the vehicle route that links up with the island's road. The walk will return alongside these arrows, but for now, keep further to the right,

Walking across the sandy causeway to the tidal islet of Illaunakeegher.

passing north of the rocks in the centre of the strand and heading towards the cemetery that can be seen on the opposite shore.

The cemetery is still in use today by local inhabitants. Turn right in front of the graveyard, and begin to follow the coast in an anticlockwise direction. The first landmark is a prominent white house at the north-eastern corner of the island; walk across the sandy, rock-studded shore and pass beneath the building. As you turn the corner the view opens up to the west, along the channel that separates Omey from Aughrus Point. A pier can be seen partway along the channel's northern shore, while open ocean surges at the mouth of the inlet.

A couple of hundred metres beyond the white house, cross a small stream and climb a grassy hummock, which is actually an old midden site. Drop back to the beach, then look for a place where the fence on the left turns inland. Follow this fence for 50m to view the remains of Teampall Féichín, or St Feichin's Church. This medieval church is constructed from pink granite blocks, and occupies the site of an earlier monastic settlement. It lies within a machair hollow, and was only rediscovered in 1981 when shifting sands revealed a protruding gable wall.

Return to the beach and turn left to resume your journey along the shore. In recent years, coastal erosion has cut into the land here, creating a cliff of sand up to 5m high and 100m long at the back of the beach. As the land has receded, numerous archaeological deposits have been exposed, including ancient human bones that were once part of a medieval graveyard.

As you continue west along the coast, you can choose between walking along the shore, or striding easily across the short grass above. The entire north-western portion of Omey consists of open machair, and walkers can roam freely and easily wherever they like. The island narrows to a sharp point at its north-western tip, and as you approach the headland, there are simultaneous views across both the northern channel and the west coast. The west is far more exposed to Atlantic swells, and is likely to have more waves rolling in to shore.

Continue right to the tip of the island. The tidal islet of Illaunakeegher lies just offshore here, and it is worth heading out to the prominent stone cairn that marks its centre. This vantage point allows great 360° views, both back over Omey and across the numerous islands that decorate the Atlantic horizon. Cruach Island lies to the west, the distinctive rock fangs on its northern shore silhouetted against the skyline. High Island can also be seen to the north-west; it contains the remains of another seventh-century monastery established by St Feichin, and was once linked to Omey through the regular transfer of goods and monks.

Omey's western shore is a jumble of rocks, and the easiest walking terrain is along the machair above the shore. Follow the coast south to a deep bay that extends inland. The view east from here is quite lovely, across the sandy beach at the back of the bay, with the Twelve Ben mountains rising majestically behind.

It is worth making a short detour away from the coast now, and heading inland to the stone cairn that can be seen sitting atop a rock outcrop. This modest rise is Omey's highest point, and makes a great place to survey the island as a whole.

Retrace your steps back to the coast, heading towards a mound of stones that lies partway along the inlet. This is St Feichin's holy well, whose retaining wall is a treasure trove of votive offerings. The spring has run dry, but this is still a place of pilgrimage for people seeking a cure for all manner of physical ailments.

Continue past another midden site to the beach, which is known as Trá Rabhach, or 'The Fruitful Strand'. Around two thirds of the way along

Votive offerings decorate the walls of St Feichin's holy well.

the sand, turn inland and join a sandy track. Follow this for 200m to the narrow strip of tarmac that is Omey's only road. Turn left here and follow the road for 1.5km. Along the way you pass Fahy Lough – home to a variety of swans and ducks – and a scattering of small farms and cottages, many of which are still in use but not as primary dwellings.

The road carries you easily back to Omey Strand. Follow the signs across the sand to return to the mainland car park.

Grade:	3
Time:	3–4 hours
Distance:	10.5km (6½ miles)
Ascent:	100m (330ft)
Map:	OSi 1:50,000 sheet 51, or OSi 1:25,000 *Oileáin Árann – The Aran Islands*.

ROUTE 17
Inisheer

Limestone pavement and ancient ruins abound on this fascinating circumnavigation of the smallest Aran Island.

Start & Finish: The route starts and finishes at Inisheer ferry pier (grid reference: L979030). Ferries run here from both Rossaveal, 37km west of Galway city, and from Doolin in County Clare.

The crossing from Rossaveal can take up to one hour and costs €25 return. Ferries run daily throughout the year. For full schedule details, contact **Aran Island Ferries** (Tel: 091 568 903; www.aranislandferries.com).

Ferries from Doolin operate daily from March to October. The crossing takes 30 minutes and costs €20 return. Try **Doolin2Aran Ferries** (Tel: 065 707 5949; www.doolin2aranferries.com) or **Doolin Ferry** (Tel: 065 707 5555; doolinferry.com).

All sailings are subject to weather and sea conditions, so always check with your ferry operator before travelling.

Inisheer (or Inis Oírr) lies 8km off the coast of County Clare. At just 3km by 2.5km, it is the smallest of the three Aran Islands, but in many ways offers the best walking. Its rocky, barren landscape, maze of stone-walled fields and host of historic sites perfectly encapsulate the exposed and ancient atmosphere that pervades all three islands. Yet Inisheer

Stone walls are one of the defining characteristics of the Aran Islands. Courtesy Tony Kirby

is also quiet, offers more off-road opportunities for exploration, and is the perfect size for a complete circumnavigation to fit neatly into a day trip.

The limestone pavement that underpins the island is a continuation of the karst landscape of the Burren, on the mainland. During the summer,

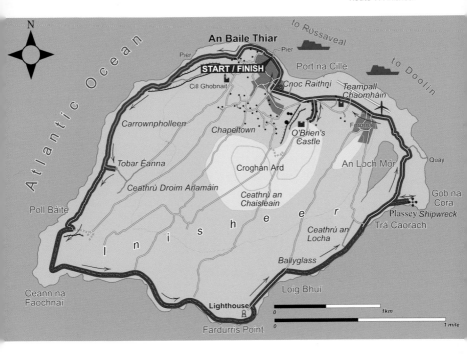

a similar array of miniature wildflowers can be seen hiding in the crevices between the rocks. The profusion of stone and lack of trees give the island a distinctly remote and windswept feel, yet people have lived in communities here for at least 5,000 years. Today Inisheer is a Gaeltacht island – meaning Irish is the first language spoken – and the population numbers around 260 permanent inhabitants.

Inisheer has two signed loop walks, but – like the marked walks on all three Aran Islands – these are confined to the roads around the main village and fail to uncover the island's wilder charms. This route explores further afield. It does include around 3km along quiet lanes, but the remainder of the circuit is spent following gravel tracks or crossing open, rocky shelves above the shore. The route is unsigned, though you do meet the purple and green arrows of the loop walks near the island's northern shore.

Though the terrain is largely flat, supportive footwear is recommended to help cross the rocks along the coastal sections.

The Walk

From the ferry pier, turn right along the narrow road above the shore. At the next junction turn right again, passing South Aran House and continuing to the small fishing pier at the north-west corner of the island.

Continue to follow the lane, which has a gravel surface now, along Inisheer's west coast. There are good views west to Inishmaan, and the coastal landscape consists of exposed limestone punctuated by occasional green fields. If the fields seem slightly incongruous amid the grey rock, that's because they are. Most of these pastures were created through centuries or even millennia of human effort. First the rocks were cleared and built into the mosaic of high stone walls that are so characteristic of the Aran Islands. Then a mixture of seaweed and sand was carried up from the shore to create fertile soil. Back-breaking work, and just one of the many challenges of living in such an isolated and barren environment.

Continue along the track, past an acute-angled junction where you join the purple arrows of one of the island's loop walks. About 1km beyond the acute junction, turn left along a tarmac lane. Just 100m later you arrive at Tobar Éanna, a holy well dedicated to St Enda. This natural spring never runs dry and is believed to have healing powers.

Return to the coast and continue south, along what is now a rough track. The marked loop walk soon turns left, but you should continue ahead along the coast. When the track peters out, head south across the limestone pavement and strips of grass to reach the southern shore.

Pass around the headland of Ceann na Faochnaí in the island's south-western corner, then follow the coast east. A gently sloping, limestone platform above the shore provides a relatively easy walking surface, though you will need to watch out for fissures in the rock.

Views of the Cliffs of Moher beckon you towards the prominent, striped lighthouse at Fardurris Point. The lighthouse was built in 1857 and is now uninhabited. Walk around the enclosing wall and use a stile to cross another wall by the entrance gate. Now back on a level surface, follow the gravel approach lane north-east between stone walls.

After 500m you reach a place where the wall on the right disappears, allowing access to the coast again. Turn right here and follow a rough track just below the fields, with open shoreline on your right.

The track consolidates as you progress up the island's east coast. As you approach the headland of Gob na Cora, the rusty hulk of a shipwrecked cargo ship looms ever larger on the rocks ahead. This is the *Plassey*, a freighter that was driven onshore by a storm in March 1960. Some sixty islanders assisted local lifeboat crews with the rescue operation, and all eleven crewmembers were saved. Tigh Ned's pub, near the ferry pier, displays a collection of photographs and documents relating to the rescue.

From the wreck, retrace your steps back along the track for 100m, then turn right onto a lane. Here you rejoin the green and purple arrows of the marked loop walks. Follow the road around Inisheer's north-eastern corner, passing Loch Mór, the island's only freshwater lake, on the way.

Soon you reach the airstrip on your right. Near the end of the runway, in a sunken pit on the left side of the road, you will find Teampall Chaomháin, or the Church of St Keevaun. This small tenth-century church is dedicated to the island's patron saint, and is remarkably intact considering it was buried under sand until its rediscovery the nineteenth century. It is surrounded by the island's graveyard, which contains St Keevaun's grave as well as more modern headstones and Celtic crosses. The mass of shells at the entrance to the graveyard was a kitchen midden during Early Christian or Medieval times.

At the next junction after Teampall Chaomháin, turn left. Climb along the road for 250m to reach the ruins of fifteenth-century Caisleán Uí Bhríain, or O'Brien's Castle. Though now in ruins, this was once an imposing, three-storey tower house built within the Stone Age fort of Dún Formna. It was the seat of the O'Brien dynasty, which ruled the island during the Middle Ages. Even now it remains the most prominent structure on the island, and its elevated position provides fine views across much of Inisheer.

Return to the coast road. If the weather is good, it is hard to avoid the temptation to cross straight over the road and follow a track to the beach. This sandy cove provides sheltered swimming, and is popular with families during the summer. To return directly to the ferry pier from here, cross to the slipway at the western side of the beach and follow the shore road for 150m.

If you want to add one final antiquity to the route, return to the road at the back of the beach and turn right. At the next T-Junction you will notice a circular mound on the right, with two vertical stones in the centre. This is Cnoc Raithní, a two-tier burial mound that provides the earliest visible evidence of civilisation on the island. The lower tier dates from the Early Bronze age, around 1500 BC, while the upper level was added during from the Early Christian period.

Turn right at the T-junction, then left at the slipway, and follow the coast road back to the pier where the route began.

The Plassey *was shipwrecked during a storm in 1960. Courtesy Tony Kirby*

ROUTE 18

Black Head

Grade:	4
Time:	4½–5½ hours
Distance:	14.5km (9 miles)
Ascent:	410m (1,350ft)
Map:	OSi 1:50,000 sheet 51

Exposed limestone pavement, archaeological sites and fine coastal views all feature on this unusual circuit in the Burren.

Start & Finish: The route starts and finishes at the large car park beside St Patrick's Church in Fanore (grid reference: O270188). Fanore is located along the R477 coast road between Doolin and Ballyvaughan in County Clare. St Patrick's Church is signed 150m along the Khyber Pass road near the northern end of the village.

The Burren is renowned for its limestone geology, and the bare, terraced domes visited on this route are a classic example of the landscape of the region. The rock formations combine with archaeological sites and fabulous views across Galway Bay to make walking here a unique and memorable experience.

The limestone itself is around 340 million years old, and began life as marine deposits on the floor of a tropical sea, back when the Irish land mass resided near the equator. After the sea retreated the rock was covered

Limestone pavement and wildflowers typical of the Burren landscape.

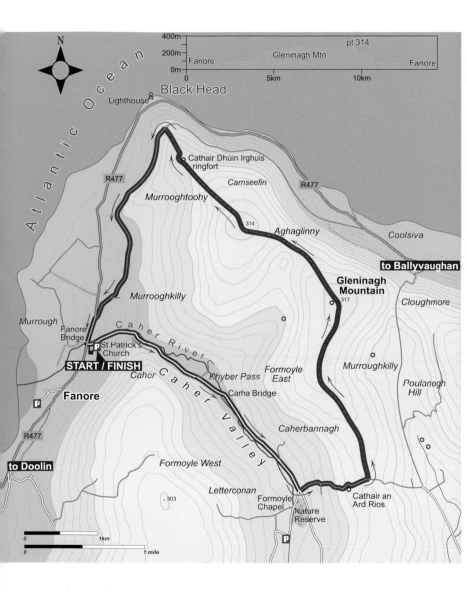

The limestone is riven with water-worn fissures.

by soil, but subsequent erosion, accelerated by the clearance of trees by early farmers, has left what now looks like a rock desert. Incredibly, the limestone here is up to 780m thick, and covers an area of 250 square kilometres. The pavement is broken every few inches by water-worn fissures, leaving an intriguing maze of rock ledges for you to balance across. From April to July each year the scene becomes even more fascinating, as the cracks fill up with a profusion of colourful wildflowers, creating miniature displays that enthral casual and expert botanists alike.

This circuit begins with 3.5km along a minor road, but follows small tracks and open hillside for the remainder of the route. The 317m summit of Gleninagh Mountain provides the modest highpoint, and a second peak is crossed before you descend to one of the finest archaeological sites in the region: the Iron Age fort of Cathair Dhúin Irghuis. As well as unique rock formations, fantastic coastal views are a feature throughout. It is also worth keeping an eye open for herds of wild goats, which can sometimes be seen roaming the area.

One word of caution: the rocky maze under your feet may be intriguing, but the fissures between the stones are potentially hazardous. Take care when placing your feet to avoid turning an ankle.

The Walk

From the entrance to St Patrick's Church, turn right onto the road. The road is known as the Khyber Pass and it follows the line of the Caher River. This is only surface river in the Burren: all other streams seep through cracks in the limestone and flow underground, through a subterranean underworld that contains more active river caves than any other part of Ireland.

Climb steadily along the tarmac for 3.5km. Traffic is light and the rapids to your left provide distraction. Eventually you reach a road junction, where waymarking posts indicate the route of the Burren Way. Continue ahead for another few metres, then turn left onto a winding stone track that is also signed as part of the Burren Way.

Climb along the track, past a collection of old farm buildings and the ruined fort of Cathair an Aird Rios on the right. Leave the track at the top of the hill, cross a stone wall on the left and strike out across open ground. The conspicuous green mound of Gleninagh Mountain is visible to the north, and the route veers north-west and then north-east along a rounded ridge to reach it. The ground underfoot is a mixture of grass and limestone pavement, and you will have to cross several stone walls along the way.

The summit of Gleninagh is marked by a trig pillar. Panoramic views encompass Galway Bay to the north, as well as many of the surrounding rock-terraced hills that are so typical of the Burren. The next goal is the unnamed summit of 314m that lies to the north-west. To get there, begin by descending along a ridge to a col. During the descent you may find your way blocked by several short cliffs, but these are easily overcome by skirting along the top of each obstacle until you find a point of weakness where you can descend more easily.

Herds of wild goats can sometimes be seen roaming the area.

Once in the col, keep close to a wall that runs along its north-eastern edge. The ground underfoot is almost exclusively limestone now, and the rocky pavement continues for the remainder of the mountain section. Climb north-east to reach the large cairn that marks the unnamed summit. This cairn is known as Dobhach Brainin and archaeologists believe it may be of Neolithic origin. The coastal views are even better here, with the three Aran Islands taking centre stage amid a wider Atlantic panorama covering much of Clare and Galway.

Descend north-west from the unnamed summit, skirting around several more cliff-like terraces on the way. The circular stone walls of Cathair Dhúin Irghuis now come into sight ahead. Cross another couple of walls to reach the fort, which once may have been the seat of a Celtic king. It measures 25m in diameter by 4m high, and is one of roughly 400 ring forts that lie scattered across the Burren region.

Continue past the fort for another 500m to reach an old green road, where a grassy track is enclosed within stone walls. Turn left here and follow the track south-west towards Fanore, passing several more stone walls along the way. The fields alongside the track often contain Connemara ponies, beautiful animals full of character that are native to Ireland.

Near the end of the green road you will find progress blocked by a jumble of rocks. Cross into the field on the left to avoid the obstacle. Now cross a final wall and join a gravel track, which leads downhill to a junction with the R477. Turn left here and follow the tarmac for 400m, then turn left again. You are now back on the Khyber Pass road, with St Patrick's Church just ahead on the right.

ROUTE 19
Cliffs of Moher

Grade:	2
Time:	3½–4½ hours
Distance:	13km (8 miles)
Ascent:	240m (790ft)
Map:	OSi 1:50,000 sheets 51 and 57

This linear path passes above Ireland's most famous sea cliffs, with magnificent coastal scenery throughout.

Start & Finish: The route starts in Doolin village in County Clare. Either park in a long lay-by just west of the bridge over the Aille River in Fisher Street (grid reference: R068965), or 1km further north-west along the R479 at Doolin Community Centre. The walk finishes at a large car park beside Moher Sports Field, just south-east of Hag's Head (grid reference: R027885). See the introduction below for details of bus services back to the start.

For most people, the Cliffs of Moher need no introduction. One of the most spectacular stretches of vertical cliff line in the country, it is a Signature Discovery Point of the Wild Atlantic Way, and home to a visitor centre that attracts almost a million visitors annually. The people come to gaze across an Atlantic rock face that stretches for over 8km at more than 100m high, and reaches its highest point – some 214m – just north of the tourist centre.

Summer daisies line the top of the cliffs.

Hiker dwarfed by the cliffs, with O'Brien's Tower in the distance.

Visiting the cliffs has been popular for centuries, but it was 2013 before an official through-path was opened along the top of the precipice. This suddenly offered walkers a fabulous opportunity to explore the entire 14km stretch of coastline between Doolin and Hag's Head, allowing them to experience the coast's quieter charms as well as the busy stretch around the visitor centre.

As with all linear routes, you do have to think about transport logistics to get back to the start. If you do not have a second vehicle, consider using Bus Éireann's service No. 350, which travels between Doolin, the Cliffs of Moher Visitor Centre and Liscannor, between three and five times daily. For full timetable information, see www.buseireann.ie or call the Galway bus office on 091 562 000. The bus can collect or deposit you along the R478, around 1.5km from the finish at Moher Sports Field (see the final paragraph of the route description for walking directions). The sharp turn at grid reference R043888 is a good place to hop on or off, but be aware that buses stop here on request only, so you will need to flag it down or arrange a special drop-off with the driver.

The route forms part of the 114km-long Burren Way. It is well signed throughout and follows an obvious trail that is constructed in most places. Be warned, however – much of the route passes along the edge of a sheer drop, with nothing to protect you from the gaping abyss below. Avoid walking in high winds and exercise extreme caution near the cliff edge.

The Walk

Begin at the road junction on the eastern side of the Aille River bridge in Fisher Street, Doolin. From here, follow the road that climbs south-west. At the top of the rise, the road veers left and a track continues straight ahead. The junction is marked by an information board for the Burren Way.

Pass around a metal gate and follow the track ahead. Already there are fine views west over the Clare coastline to the Aran Islands. Just before a second gate, turn right and climb across two stiles. This brings you to the edge of the cliffs, where you turn left and begin to follow the coastline south. Join a gravel footpath that runs between a fence and the top of the cliffs. The coast here consists of a series of rock slabs and angular ledges, and after 500m you pass the archaeological remains of a portal tomb in a field on the left. An adjacent stile provides access and allows you to explore the site fully.

The path now veers inland slightly and climbs across a hillside to reach a higher section of cliff. Despite the increasing drop on the seaward side of the path, there are no safety barriers between the trail and the edge of the precipice. The result is a wild and thrilling experience, but please take care near the edge.

Enjoying one of the most spectacular stretches of vertical cliff line in the country.

Continue ahead, passing above Aillenasharragh, which hosts some of the biggest wave surfing in Europe when large Atlantic swells push in from the west. The next landmark is an open field, where the constructed trail disappears underfoot. Signs direct you along a fence to a cattle pen at the top of the field. Squeeze along the right hand side of the pen to reach a track near the R478 road.

Rejoin the constructed pathway and turn right across another field to return to the cliff top. Here, at a lofty vantage point, the first, breathtaking view across the main cliffs is suddenly revealed. The precipice is now over 200m high – the highest point of the entire route – and the rock face is plumb vertical or even undercut.

You are now approaching the Cliffs of Moher Visitor Centre and may begin to pass more people along the trail. You enter the grounds themselves at a paved area surrounding O'Brien's Tower, a viewing point that dates from 1835.

The path is heavily constructed now, with a protective line of stone slabs on the seaward side. Descend to a hollow; the visitor centre, with its exhibitions, toilets, gift shop and café, is located a short distance to the left here. The coastal route continues ahead, following a brief stretch of tarmac before the footpath resumes at the top of the hill. The view is still incredible, with 5km of thrusting headlands and magnificent cliff line visible between O'Brien's Tower and Hag's Head.

As you exit the southern end of the visitor centre grounds, the trail dwindles to an unprotected, earthen footpath. The cliffs gradually lose height now, though there are plenty more good views all the way to Hag's Head. This headland is crowned by Moher Tower, a partially ruined, Napoleonic signal tower that was built in the early 1800s. It is worth pausing here for a moment to explore the tower and savour the final coastal views of the route.

When you're ready, follow the path that leads inland from the back of the tower. Descend to the end of a stone track, then continue onto a tarmac lane. You now pass a private, fee-paying car park on the right, which provides the closest parking to Hag's Head. Moher Sports Field, with its large, free car park, is located on the left some 800m further along the road.

If you plan to use Bus Éireann's service No. 350 to return to the start, continue south along the road from Moher Sports Field. Turn left at a T-junction, still following signs for the Burren Way. Walk straight ahead along this road for 1.5km, continuing past the point where the Burren Way turns off. This brings you to directly to the R478, where you can hail the bus back to Doolin.

ROUTE 20
Loop Head

Grade:	3
Time:	2½–3½ hours
Distance:	10.5km (6½ miles)
Ascent:	120m (390ft)
Map:	OSi 1:50,000 sheet 63

This varied circuit takes you along the top of dramatic cliffs and right to the western tip of County Clare.

Start & Finish: The walk starts and finishes at a large car park beside Loop Head Lighthouse (grid reference: Q691472). Begin by heading to the village of Kilkee. From here follow signs to Loop Head, some 26km south-west along the R487. The lighthouse and car park are located at the end of the road along the peninsula.

Loop Head marks the point where Ireland's greatest river finally concedes to the sea. With the Shannon estuary lying to the south of the headland and the Atlantic Ocean to the north, the tip of this long, tapering peninsula is a natural focus of curiosity. Little wonder it is celebrated as one of the Signature Discovery Points of the Wild Atlantic Way.

The north coast of Loop Head is particularly interesting, its border defined by a variety of natural rock architecture including sea stacks, arches and sheer cliffs up to 60m high. This walk takes you past the best scenery and offers fine coastal views too: on a clear day the Aran Islands and mountains of Connemara can both be seen to the north.

Loop Head Lighthouse was built in 1854.

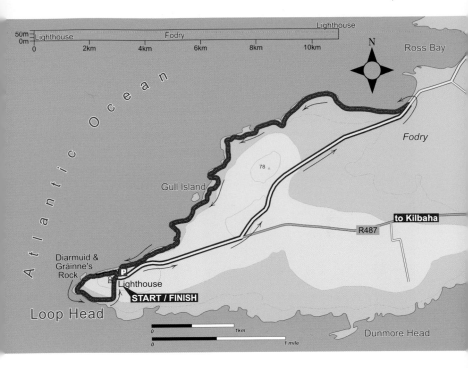

The route begins with 4km of quiet laneway, then doubles back along the top of open cliffs. The walk is not signed, but navigation is straightforward throughout. The only note of caution concerns the need to take care near the cliff edge.

As you explore the area it is worth keeping an eye open for wildlife. Loop Head is home to thousands of nesting seabirds during the summer months, and is one of Europe's best bird-watching sites for migratory species too. It is also a favourite location for whale and dolphin spotters: Europe's largest pod of bottlenose dolphins, numbering over 160 individuals, lives here at the mouth of the Shannon.

It is also possible to combine this walk with a guided tour of Loop Head Lighthouse. Inside you will find an exhibit detailing the building's history, and there's an opportunity to climb the tower and walk around the balcony at the top. The lighthouse is open from April to September, and entrance costs €5 per person.

At the time of writing, three new loop walks were also being developed around Loop Head, and these should be complete by late 2016. More choice is generally a good thing, so if you're walking after that date, you may want to check the new route options too.

The cliffs include several dramatic rock formations.

The Walk

Loop Head has long been a nautical landmark for shipping traffic up and down the Shannon estuary. The first lighthouse was established here in 1670, and consisted of a fire lit on the roof of the lightkeeper's cottage. The present tower was built in 1854 and automated in 1991, while the lightkeepers' houses have now been turned into holiday homes.

From the car park, begin by heading along the road away from the lighthouse. The first section allows tantalising glimpses of the cliffs to the left, but you will have to wait until the end of the route to explore the coastline fully.

Roughly 1.5km from the lighthouse, turn left onto a lane signed as the 'Coast Road'. This road provides simultaneous views over both the Atlantic to the north and the gaping mouth of the Shannon to the south. Descend gradually along the lane, past green fields and an interesting array of farms and cottages, one with a rather eclectic display of marine flotsam in the garden. Veer left at the bottom of the hill to reach Ross Bay, which often has heaving lines of swell rolling in from the west.

Ross Bay is surrounded by rounded stones. Leave the road here and turn sharp left, climbing over the rocks piled at the back of the bay and heading west along the coast. This is the only place on the route where you draw level with the water, so it is a natural location for a short break.

When you're ready, join a strip of grass between the edge of the fields and the shore. Progress around the back of the bay is slightly awkward in places, but the grass becomes shorter, and the walking space wider, as you leave the bay and continue west.

The shoreline rocks grow inexorably higher and wilder as you make your way along the coast. The first landmarks are two bulbous inlets, which you must veer around. As you pass beneath the hill marked on the map as 78m, the fields on your left come to an end and you find yourself walking along the edge of wild, open grassland.

One of the headlands is undermined by a massive rock arch.

The lighthouse soon comes into view ahead, then a sheer drop heralds the beginning of the cliffs proper. The precipice is high and vertical from now on, so please take care near the edge. An impressive rock arch lies at the start of the section, followed by Gull Island and a labyrinth of stacks and ridges teetering on the edge of a sloping ledge. The next sheer-sided bay is a favourite summer nesting spot for guillemots and razorbills, as the sight and smell of guano-covered ledges will attest. If you look back from the far side of this bay, you will also see that this entire headland is actually undermined by a massive rock arch, which waves crash right through in big swells.

The cliffs remain plumb vertical all the way to the lighthouse. Follow the path along the top of the precipice, passing to the right of the lighthouse compound and continuing towards the tip of Loop Head. You will soon reach a spot known as Lovers' Leap, beside a sea stack called Diarmuid & Gráinne's Rock. These names relate to one of the most enduring tales of Irish mythology: the two lovers eloped together and were pursued by Gráinne's jilted fiancé, the great warrior leader Fionn mac Cumhaill. It is said that the couple leapt onto this rock in desperation to escape the band of soldiers chasing them. The cairn on top of the stack has more recent origins, however; it was erected in 1990 by two climbers who abseiled down the cliffs, then climbed across to the summit.

Also near the end of Loop Head, you will notice the word 'Eire' written on the ground in white stones. This is a relic of the Second World War, designed to alert passing pilots to the fact that neutral Ireland lay below. Nearby, between the stones and the lighthouse, is a ruined concrete lookout post, where staff from the local Coast Watching Service monitored wartime activity in the surrounding ocean.

Right at the very tip of the peninsula is a high rock shelf. It is an exhilarating experience to stand here watching the waves crash below, and imagine that the next land west is North America, over 3,000km away.

Return to the car park by following a grassy trail along the southern side of the headland, enjoying fine views south to Brandon Mountain and the undulating spine of the Dingle Peninsula. Pass along the white wall that surrounds the lighthouse. A final left turn alongside the wall will bring you back to the car park where the route began.

Follow a strip of grass along the southern side of the headland..

ROUTE 21

Magharee Peninsula

Grade:	2
Time:	4–5 hours
Distance:	15km (9½ miles)
Ascent:	30m (100ft)
Map:	OSi 1:50,000 sheet 71

Explore a series of sandy beaches on this easy circuit around Ireland's largest tombolo.

Start & Finish: The route starts and finishes at the car park for Castlegregory Beach (grid reference: Q626139) in County Kerry. Castlegregory is usually approached via the R560. Continue through the village centre, then turn right at an off-set crossroads, following a sign for the local GAA club. The large car park is located at the end of the road.

If you prefer a shorter route, you also start and finish at a car park above Sandy Bay (grid reference: Q618162). From Castlegregory, continue straight ahead at the off-set crossroads, following signs for Kilshannig and Fahamore. The car park is located 3km later on the right.

This is a perfect route for anyone who loves beaches: over 15km of walking, of which more than 11km is along the sand. The final strand, Magherabeg Beach, is also the longest beach in Ireland.

Yet the route has variety too, visiting three distinct bays on its circuit around the Magharee Peninsula. The north-eastern tip of the peninsula is particularly atmospheric, the traditional cottages and free-roaming livestock creating an impression of time gone by. The peninsula is actually Ireland's largest tombolo, a sandy ridge that connects a previously detached island to the mainland. In geological terms the land here is very new, having been built by accumulated ocean sediment over the past 10,000 years. It now forms a significant geographical landmark, separating Brandon Bay to the west from Tralee Bay to the east.

Much of the route follows the Dingle Way, a long-distance walking trail that circumnavigates the Dingle Peninsula. The marker posts are sporadic, however, so do not be surprised if you walk several kilometres without seeing one. The terrain is flat and easy, and lightweight shoes are quite sufficient. In some places the exact route you take will be dictated by the tide; at low water you can stroll freely along wide, sandy flats, while at high tide you may be forced onto the land above. Use your common sense, and enjoy a memorable walk around a unique coastal feature. For a shorter route, start and finish at the car park above Sandy Bay to save 5km.

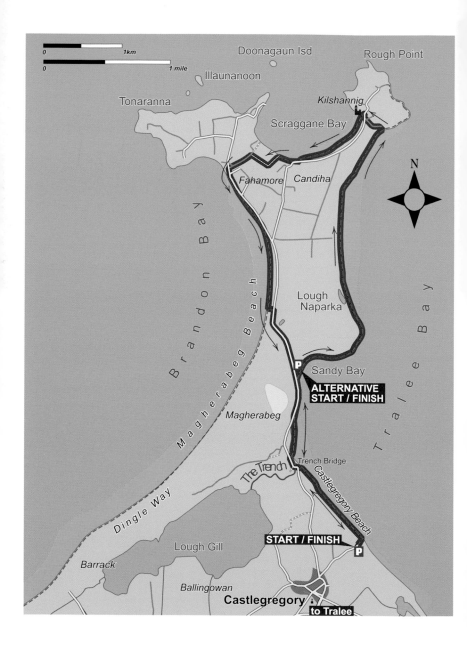

Sandy Bay provides great views of the Slieve Mish mountains.

The Walk

From the car park, drop onto Castlegregory Beach, turn left, and begin heading north along the sand. The beach consists predominately of sand, with a scattering of pebbles, scallop shells, mother-of-pearl oyster inlays and other natural treasures. After 1.5km you reach The Trench, the outlet river that drains Lough Gill, which is too deep to cross easily. Avoid the obstacle by turning left 250m before the river, and following a sandy trail through the dunes to the road.

Turn right onto the road and cross the bridge, then return to the beach on the opposite side. At low tide it is possible to follow the beach for the next 2km, but at high tide you will be forced across some boulders and back onto the road for 600m. Continue beside the tarmac to a mobile home park and lifeguard hut, then turn right and drop back down to the shore at Sandy Bay. This sheltered spot is popular with holidaymakers, with all sorts of water-based activities taking place in summer. The car park here also offers an alternative start/finish point for walkers who prefer a shorter circuit.

You are now on the route of the Dingle Way, which you follow for the next 8km. Head east around Sandy Bay; despite its name the beach here is predominately stony, but it does provide great views south to the peaks of the Slieve Mish mountains. Follow the coast as it sweeps north, where firm, boulder-studded sand returns underfoot. Continue across 3km of

Two friends roam along the beach near Kilshannig.

wide, flat sand, heading towards the clustered houses of Kilshannig at the northern tip of the strand. Your journey may be enlivened by a group of friendly horses, who roam freely along this coast.

Around 700m before Kilshannig you can choose to divert onto a common of short grass at the back of the beach. You may see a herd of cattle grazing here, and again it is lovely to see animals wandering freely in such a beautiful setting. Continue towards the end of the beach, to a prominent white house with a Dingle Way marker in front of it. This route makes a small detour here; ignore the marker and turn left instead, following a track inland beside a stone wall.

The track brings you to a road where you should turn right, then quickly left again beside a picturesque cottage named 'Josie's'. You are now in Scraggane Bay, a fine, horseshoe-shaped cove at the northern tip of

Pass picturesque Josie's cottage to reach Scraggane Bay.

the Magharee Peninsula. The Magharee Islands – or Seven Hogs as they are also known – lie scattered just offshore. All the islands are uninhabited now, but local farmers still use them for summer grazing. The sheep and cattle used to swim across to the islands, but much of the drama has been taken out of the crossing thanks to a floating animal cage that can be pulled behind a boat.

Head west along the sand, with the harbour at Scraggane Point ahead. Just before a cluster of houses, clamber up some boulders to reach the road above. The road veers inland here, but you should follow a Dingle Way sign onto a track between the beach and a house. Take care now, because the next turn was unmarked at the time of writing. Follow a footpath around the seaward side of one field, then drop into an overgrown, ditch-like boreen with old stone walls and electric fences on either side. Turn left here and head inland along a narrow, grassy path. At the end of the field turn right. The path widens and brings you to a track, where you should turn left.

You emerge onto a road at the side of Spillane's Bar. Turn left and follow the road for 150m, then descend across boulders onto the northern end of Magherabeg Beach. This is Ireland's longest beach, sweeping around the back of Brandon Bay for 11km, with Brandon Mountain towering over its western end. This side of the Magharee Peninsula is much more exposed to Atlantic swells than the east, and there are often lines of thunderous waves crashing onto the strand. No surprise then that this a popular destination for surfers, and in favourable conditions you may well be entertained by their acrobatic manoeuvres as you make your way along the beach.

Follow the sand south for 2km, then look for an access point through the dunes to the road. The easiest place is at a wide sandy track, marked on the seaward side by a dune erosion sign and an orange ring buoy. Head up the track, past several cabins belonging to local surf schools, to reach the road beyond.

Turn right and follow the road for just over 1km, until you return to the eastern side of the peninsula. Here you should recognise your surroundings from your outward journey. Drop back onto Castlegregory Beach where possible and complete the final stretch back to the start.

Walking along Castlegregory Beach at the start of the route.

ROUTE 22

Brandon Mountain

Grade:	5
Time:	4½–5½ hours
Distance:	9km (5½ miles)
Ascent:	830m (2,720ft)
Map:	OSi 1:50,000 sheet 70, or OSi 1:25,000 Brandon Mountain.

This out-and-back ascent lets you appreciate the fabulous coastal views from one of Ireland's most captivating mountains.

Start & Finish: The route starts and finishes at a car park in Faha, just northwest of the village of Cloghane (grid reference: Q494119) in County Kerry. Begin by heading to Cloghane, which can either be reached via the Conor Pass from Dingle, or via the N86 and R560 from Tralee. From Cloghane, continue north along the R585 for 2km, then turn left at a crossroads. The road is signed to Cnoc Bréanainn, the Irish name for Brandon Mountain. Follow the lane for 2.5km to reach the car park at the end of the road. There is space here for eight to ten vehicles.

The route provides fabulous views across Ireland's longest beach, at the back of Brandon Bay.

Brandon Mountain is renowned amongst Irish hillwalkers as one of the most charismatic peaks in the country. At 952m it is the country's ninth highest summit, and the highest outside the Iveragh Peninsula. It rises directly from the Altantic, and its location at the north-western tip of the Dingle Peninsula means its coastal views are unsurpassed.

There are several ways to reach the top, but the route described here is the most spectacular. The trip includes an approach along a wild ridge, a climb between the towering rock battlements of

Enjoying a winter view across the west Dingle coast from just below Brandon's summit.

a glacial corrie, a sudden exit onto the roof of the Dingle Peninsula, and summit views that sweep from Ireland's highest mountains to the azure waters off its western tip.

This is not an easy route, however. The difficulty of the terrain and the effort required to reach the top mean it has more in common with a mountain route than a coastal walk, and the outing is best left to those with previous hillwalking experience. Navigation is relatively straightforward because the route follows a rough path that is marked for most of the way, but you should still carry the full OSi map. Care is needed along the edge of a cliff near the summit, and vertigo sufferers might not appreciate the steep climb out of the corrie.

Brandon is named after St Brendan, an early monastic saint who was born in AD 484 and became one of the Twelve Apostles of Ireland. Known as Brendan the Navigator, he is most famed for his legendary voyage to the 'Isle of the Blessed'. Along with a small group of pilgrims, Brendan set out from the coast of Kerry in a currach, a small, traditional boat. His subsequent journey around the Atlantic lasted up to nine years, and is described in hundreds of medieval manuscripts. It is sometimes hard to separate fact from legend, but many scholars believe Brendan made it at least as far as Iceland, probably to Greenland, and possibly even to North America.

St Brendan is reputed to have climbed to the summit of Brandon Mountain before setting out on his epic journey, praying for safe passage and meditating on the journey ahead. Modern pilgrims still flock to the

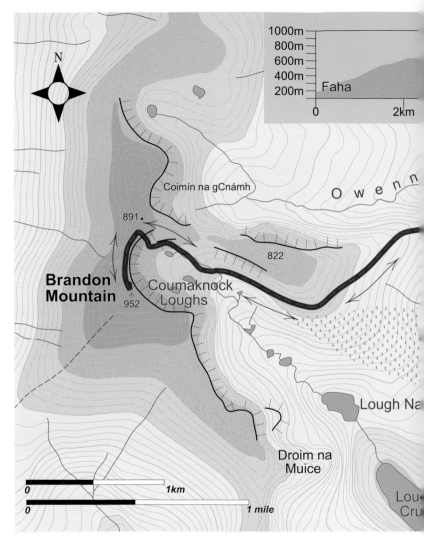

summit in memory of the saint, climbing the peak via the Saints Road, a path that ascends the south-western flanks of the mountain.

One final word of warning: Brandon's coastal location makes it susceptible to cloud cover and high winds driven in from the sea. Watch the forecast carefully to avoid walking in bad weather, both because of the dangers of confronting precipitous terrain in poor visibility, and because it would be a shame to miss out on the views.

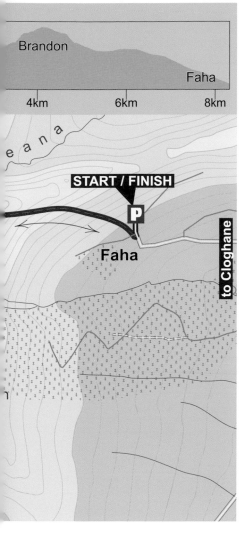

The Walk

From Faha, join a grassy track that starts from the top right corner of the car park. Follow the signs and pass through a gate. On the other side of the gate lies open mountain terrain, with a sign that indicates the ascent route to Brandon. Join a stony path marked by a series of white poles. This leads past a well-tended grotto, then climbs diagonally along the shoulder ahead. Already there are fabulous views east across Ireland's longest beach, which sweeps around the back of Brandon Bay, and further afield across the Dingle Peninsula.

As you round a ridge at the end of the shoulder, the landscape that makes Brandon so distinctive is suddenly revealed below. Hollowed out above Lough Cruite is an imposing rock corrie, with a line of paternoster lakes filling the depressions between the boulders on the basin floor. It is difficult to see how the route might escape these sheer, dark walls, and the atmosphere of the place is powerful.

The path through the corrie is marked by splashes of yellow paint. Descend to the corrie floor and follow the trail through a maze of rocks, crossing streams and passing several loughs and pools along the way. As you approach the back left corner of the corrie, the exit route becomes clear, and the path steepens significantly to zigzag up the headwall above. This is the most challenging terrain of the route. Hands are called on for support in places, and some muddy sections can be slippery when wet.

The climb is absorbing, and it is a shock to exit the corrie suddenly and find yourself atop a high ridge, with the coastline of the Dingle Peninsula

The eastern side of the Brandon Mountain massif is cut by deep glacial corries.

laid out in all its glory below. The view to the south-west is particularly impressive, across thrusting headlands and deep bays to the final outpost of the Blasket Islands.

A signpost marks the point where the corrie path joins the ridge, and it is worth making a mental note of the location so you will recognise it again on your return journey. Though the ridge is a definite milestone, the actual summit of Brandon Mountain still lies 100 vertical metres away. Turn left at the signpost and climb steadily south along the ridge, taking care to stay back from the vertical cliffs to the east.

The summit itself is decorated by a large metal cross and a stone oratory dedicated to St Brendan. There is also a magnificent 360° panorama. Closest to hand, the spectacular, cliff-fringed ridge of the Brandon massif marches south across Brandon Peak and Gearhane. Further afield, far-reaching views encompass Ireland's highest mountain range – the MacGillycuddy's Reeks on the Iveragh Peninsula – as well as the intricate mixture of farmland, coastline and hills that make up the Dingle Peninsula.

When you have fully appreciated the view, turn around and reverse your outward journey. The descent back down the headwall into the corrie demands care, then it is a relatively simple matter to retrace your steps to Faha.

Great Blasket Island

Grade:	3
Time:	3–3½ hours
Distance:	9km (5½ miles)
Ascent:	450m (1,480ft)
Map:	OSi 1:50,000 sheet 70

An evocative circuit through a deserted village and along the mountainous spine of this wild Atlantic outpost off the Kerry coast.

Start & Finish: The route starts and finishes at the landing stage on the Great Blasket Island (grid reference: V281977). Several operators provide regular ferry services to the island between Easter and September. The shortest crossing leaves from Dunquin, takes 20 minutes, and costs €30. Try **Blasket Island Boatmen** (Tel: 066 915 6422; www.blasketisland.com) or **Larry's Blasket Ferry** (Tel: 087 743 5442). A 45-minute ferry also runs from Dingle town and costs €35 – contact **Dingle Bay Charters** for details (Tel: 087 672 6100; www.dinglebaycharters.com).

All operators allow long enough on the island to complete the walk as part of a day trip. As always, phone the ferry operator before travelling to check sea conditions and departure times.

The deserted village sits above the sandy cove of An Tráigh Bhán.

Situated 2km off the tip of the Dingle Peninsula, the Blasket Islands are Ireland's most westerly land mass. Evocative, mystical islands with intriguing natural and human histories, they form one of the Signature Discovery Points of the Wild Atlantic Way.

The largest island in the archipelago, the Great Blasket, measures 6km long by 1km wide, and was inhabited until 1953. Even at its peak, the Irish-speaking fishing community that lived there never included more than 175 people. The vast majority of the land is now owned by the state, which has proposed that the island be preserved as a national park.

The experience of walking on the island is both exhilarating and memorable, and will remain etched on your mind long after you have left. The ruined stone buildings of the deserted village provide the first, poignant landmark of the route. From this atmospheric start, you climb up and along the mountainous spine of the island. Though the landscape is wild and remote, the terrain underfoot is relatively easy. Paths and tracks are followed throughout, and the route is suitable for most fit walkers.

Visitors have a high chance of seeing various species of wildlife, including seals, rabbits, seabirds, dolphins and basking sharks. To get the most out of your trip, it is also worth reading one of the celebrated,

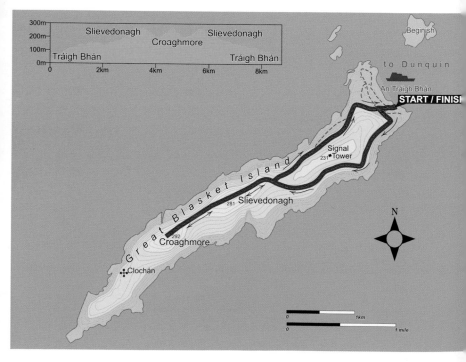

Walkers on the slopes of Slievedonagh.

first-hand accounts of life on Great Blasket – try Tomás O'Crohan's *The Islandman* for an entertaining and touching insight into life here in the late 1800s. Alternatively you could combine the walk with a visit to the Blasket Centre in Dunquin, which houses a variety of exhibits detailing the long and varied history of the islands.

It is worth waiting for good weather for this outing, both because the island has limited shelter, and because the ferry services do not operate in adverse conditions.

The Walk

Tidal fluctuations and inhospitable coastlines mean the ferry trip to the Great Blasket will probably involve at least one shuttle by inflatable dinghy, followed by a bit of hopping over wet rocks. This is all part of the fun of reaching the island, but you might want to equip yourself with an extra pair of water sandals so it doesn't matter if your feet get wet.

From the landing stage where you are deposited by the ferry, follow a grassy path up through the deserted village. The 1841 census recorded 153 people living here, in twenty-eight houses. Most of the buildings are now roofless stone ruins, though there are one or two that have been repaired in recent years.

The route begins by following a green track away from the deserted village.

Head towards the upper left corner of the settlement, where you will find a green track. Turn left here and follow the track, climbing onto the southern slopes of an unnamed hill marked on the map as point 231m. After a fairly steep initial ascent, the track evens out and contours south-west. This is an enjoyable stretch of high, easy walking, enhanced by fabulous views across to the Iveragh and Beara Peninsulas, as well as to the sharp, distant cones of the Skellig Islands.

The track climbs to the top of the ridge at the western side of the hill, where you arrive at a junction. You will head to the right here on the return journey, but for now, turn left and head west along a narrow footpath. Soon you pass the site of An Dún, an Iron Age promontory fort that dates from 800 BC. There is little to see above the ground today, but the site bears witness to the island's long history of habitation.

Continue to follow the path along the ridge, climbing through bracken to reach the broad summit of Slievedonagh (281m). Croaghmore, the highest point on the island, is now clearly visible ahead. Descend to a col, with the island narrowing inexorably around you. The northern slopes are precipitous here, and you are walking along a pleasantly narrow arête with more gentle slopes to the south.

A final climb brings you to the trig point at the 292m summit of Croaghmore. A circle of stones indicates an old clochán (beehive hut) below, and fabulous coastal views encompass the western Blasket Islands of Inishnabro and Inishvickillane.

Though it is possible to continue further south-west towards the end of the island, Croaghmore marks the turning point for most walkers. Reverse your journey along the ridge to the junction in the col just east of Slievedonagh. Turn left here and join a track that makes a gradual descent along the northern side of the island, with fine views ahead to the mountains of the Dingle Peninsula.

As you return to the eastern tip of the island, there is a fine, aerial view over the deserted village, with the beautiful sandy cove and turquoise waters of An Tráigh Bhán straight ahead. If you have any time to spare, this is a pleasurable and relaxing place to explore before you head back to the landing stage for the departure of your boat.

Herring gull in flight. Seabirds and marine mammals are frequently spotted from Great Blasket Island.

ROUTE 24

Mount Eagle

Grade: 3
Time: 3–3½ hours
Distance: 8km (5 miles)
Ascent: 500m (1,640ft)
Map: OSi 1:50,000 sheet 70

Ancient ruins, spectacular island views and a mountain summit all feature on this highly recommended route in County Kerry.

Start & Finish: The route starts and finishes at a lay-by along the R559, above Coomeenoole Bay (grid reference: V317974). The lay-by is located 3km south of Dunquin and 9km west of Ventry, and has parking space for ten cars.

It is hard to think of a route that packs more variety into 8km than this one. It is essentially a short hill walk, and includes all the sense of achievement of reaching a 516m-high summit. Yet the trip up and down the mountain's flanks includes such diversity, and is enlivened by so many fabulous views, that you can't fail to finish the route with a smile. If you are an experienced hillwalker you will find it an easy route that offers plenty of gain for very little pain, and if you are a relative novice in the hills, this is an ideal introduction to Irish mountain walking that is bound to whet your appetite for more.

Enjoying the view over Coumeenoole Bay from the lower slopes of Mount Eagle.

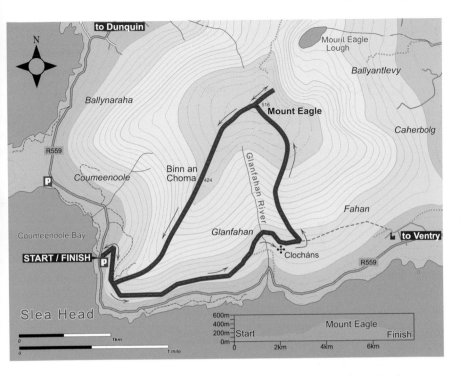

The trip begins with a stretch along the Dingle Way. This eight-day, 179km-long walking route circumnavigates the Dingle Peninsula, and forms one of the most popular long-distance trails in Ireland. The section followed here is one of the most scenic highlights of the entire trail. Little wonder: the coastal views, over Dingle Bay to the Iveragh Peninsula, and over Coumeenoole Bay to Great Blasket Island, are simply stunning.

The route has a historical context too, taking you past several ring forts and clocháns (beehive huts) belonging to the Fahan group. This is a remarkable collection of antiquities, which includes at least 460 stone forts, dwellings and monuments dating from various periods of history. Most prominent from this route are the

Stone clocháns from the Fahan community can be seen from the route.

135

The view across Mount Eagle Lough and the Dingle Peninsula from near the summit.

clocháns, some 414 of which cluster around the south-eastern slopes of Mount Eagle. Some of the earliest examples may have been built by hermit monks during Early Christian times, but most are thought to date from the twelfth century, when local farmers were forced onto marginal land by Norman invaders.

The route follows footpaths for the first and final third, but the middle section crosses open mountain. Route-finding is relatively simple but decent boots are a necessity for the upland terrain, and you will need a compass and map in poor visibility. If the idea of climbing across open mountainside seems daunting, consider an out-and-back ascent along Mount Eagle's south-west ridge. This option follows a mountain path virtually all the way, yet still allows you to appreciate the best views.

The Walk

From the lay-by, head south along the road for 60m. Look for a track on the left, guarded by a metal gate. There is a large stile beside the gate, and a waymarking post indicating the route of the Dingle Way. This is your access and exit point onto the mountain above.

Cross the stile and follow a grassy track as it zigzags up the hillside. After several hairpin bends, the track straightens out and heads south around the south-western shoulder of the hill. Here you cross another stile. The return route descends alongside the stone wall on your left, and if you want to make an out-and-back trip to the summit, you should turn left here and follow the wall up the ridge ahead. To continue on the full circuit, keep following the Dingle Way and turn right along the wall instead.

You are now following a footpath east around the base of Mount Eagle, with a stone wall on your right. There are great views south to the conical outcrops of the Skellig Islands, and south-east across Dingle Bay to the MacGillycuddy's Reeks, the highest mountain range in Ireland.

A kilometre or so beyond the stile you will begin to notice several curious stone formations in the fields below the path. These are the clocháns of the Fahan community. Each hut probably housed a whole family, with some huts attached to each other via interconnecting doorways. You will also see several larger, circular stone structures, which are old ring forts.

When the path crosses a mountain stream – the Glanfahan River – you should start to watch out for your turn off the Dingle Way. This comes roughly 400m beyond the stream, where a stone wall descends down the mountain from the left. Turn left here, and begin to climb across open hillside on the right side of the wall.

The ascent is moderately steep, and easiest if you stick to the grassy strip beside the wall and avoid rough heather elsewhere. At the top corner of the wall, climb diagonally right (north-east) towards the top of the shoulder. You now have no option but to do battle with the heather, though it is rarely more than ankle deep. As you gain height the heather turns to moorland grass, interspersed with rocks and occasional wet patches.

Great Blasket Island seen from the jagged rock outcrop of Binn an Choma.

One kilometre beyond the wall the ground evens out, and you reach the concrete trig point that marks the summit of Mount Eagle. The views are good, but for an even better panorama, head north-west for 250m to the rim of the corrie holding Mount Eagle Lough. Here you can enjoy an expanded panorama that encompasses the lake below as well as many of the mountains of the Dingle and Iveragh peninsulas, with many of Ireland's highest peaks displayed across the skyline.

When you're ready, return to the summit trig point. Now head south-west, following a line of wooden posts onto the path along the south-west shoulder. As you descend the trail consolidates underfoot, and is marked by occasional splashes of orange paint. The dominant view is now to the west, and from the upper reaches of the mountain it looks like the Great Blasket Island is a continuation of the mainland, making it easy to imagine the landscape as it might have been before Atlantic erosion separated the two pieces of land.

Follow the path along the crest of the increasingly well-defined ridge, now enjoying a really pleasurable stretch of walking. By the time you reach the jagged rock outcrop at 424m-high Binn an Choma, the view over Coumeenoole Bay is nothing short of spectacular. The beauty of this scene stays with you for the remainder of the route.

Descend to a stone enclosure and pass around its right side, ignoring an orange arrow directing you left. Follow a broken stone wall down the ridge, then, just before you pass under a power line, cross to the left side of the wall. Continue to descend alongside the wall until you reach a stile, which you should recognise from your outward journey. Turn right here, cross the stile, and retrace your initial steps back along the Dingle Way to the start.

Descending along the Dingle Way at the end of the route.

ROUTE 25
Bray Head

Grade:	3
Time:	2–2½ hours
Distance:	6km (4 miles)
Ascent:	240m (790ft)
Map:	OSi 1:50,000 sheet 83

This relatively short, signed circuit visits the most dramatic coastal scenery on Kerry's Iveragh Peninsula.

Start & Finish: The walk starts and finishes at a parking area at the south-western end of Valentia Island (grid reference: V352738). Valentia is actually connected to the mainland by a road bridge at Portmagee. Cross the bridge, then turn left at the first junction. After 1.5km turn left again, now following signs for the Looped Walk. The parking area is located on the right just a few hundred metres further west. There is parking space for at least thirty cars but even so it can be busy during peak times. The car park operates a pay-and-display system, with a flat charge of €2 at the time of writing.

B ray Head forms the western tip of Valentia Island, and is the most westerly point of the Iveragh Peninsula. In fact it is only surpassed by the tip of Dingle and a scattering of offshore islands as the most westerly land mass in Ireland. The headland itself is richly imbued with all the untamed wilderness and rugged exposure you would expect from the extremity of the Atlantic seaboard, with spectacular scenery and celebrated

The broad, stony track at the start of the Bray Head route.

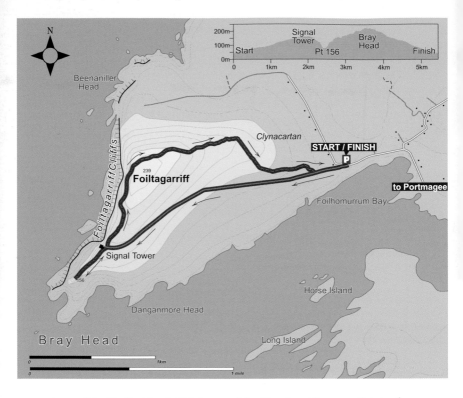

views of the Skellig Islands. This is one of the Signature Discovery Points of the Wild Atlantic Way, and it doesn't take long to appreciate why.

Bray Head is dominated by Foiltagarriff hill, which is only 239m high, but has been comprehensively and remorselessly eroded by the ocean on its western side. The result is a dramatic band of cliffs that extends almost all the way to the peaty summit. It is these cliffs that form the focal point of the walk described. For more adventurous walkers, there is an option to detour further along the ridge towards the tip of the promontory.

The route is part of a network of national loop walks, and is well signed throughout. It is one of the most popular loops in south-west Ireland, and justifiably so; it is certainly the most impressive coastal walk on the Iveragh Peninsula. It is not particularly long, but there is enough ascent to ensure a sense of achievement. A combination of tracks and footpaths provide extra navigational guidance and the ground is mostly firm underfoot, though short sections may be muddy after rain.

Besides its scenery, the name Valentia is famous throughout Ireland for two things: the weather station it lends its name to, and as the European landing point for the world's first permanent transatlantic

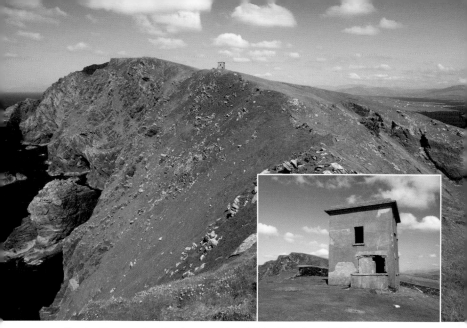

The signal tower on Bray Head was used from 1815 until the Second World War.

telecommunications link. The weather station is actually situated on the mainland just south-west of Cahersiveen, but the transatlantic cable landed at Foilhomurrum Bay, just a stone's throw from the start and finish point for this route. When it became operational in August 1858, the cable revolutionised communications between Europe and North America, reducing contact time from at least ten days to mere minutes. The importance of the cable only began to diminish in the 1960s, when alternative satellite links were established, and Valentia's Transatlantic Cable Station finally closed in 1966.

The Walk

From the entrance to the car park, turn left and follow the minor road west for 50m. This brings you to a gate with an adjacent stile. Cross the stile and head west along a broad, stony track. Almost immediately you will see an informal path, signed by waymarks, coming down the slope on the right. This is where you will rejoin the track at the end of the circuit.

For now, stay on the main track and follow it gently uphill, heading across open ground towards the signal tower that lies silhouetted on the skyline above. The ascent is around 2km long, and the track is clearly visible all the way to the tower. Fine views help to divert your attention from the effort of the climb, particularly to the south, where brooding headlands and broken fingers of rock lead the eye to Puffin Island.

Looking north along the Foiltagarriff cliffs from point 156m.

The track becomes gradually steeper and curves round to the south-west, pointing almost directly towards the twin pyramids of the Skellig Islands. Look down the slope to the left here to see the ruins of some Early Christian clocháns, or stone shelters, some of which feature rock carvings.

The track makes a final arc back to the west, then brings you to the base of the signal tower. This tower has a longer history than many such structures along the west coast. It was built during the Napoleonic Wars in 1815, but remained in use as a signal station until the 1920s and also served as a lookout post during the Second World War. Its location is nothing short of spectacular: it lies at the top of the Foiltagarriff cliffs, which plunge

The descent route features fine views across Valentia Island.

142

over 200m to the ocean just north of the building. The foreground drama is further complemented by the outline of the Dingle Peninsula and the Blasket Islands, which can be seen in the distance.

At this point confident walkers may want to detour away from the official route, and walk a little further west towards the very tip of Bray Head. The terrain on this detour is steeper and more exposed so you should exercise caution, but there is a faint, informal path underfoot. Point 156m on the OSi map is a good place to turn around, and the views back across the cliffs to the signal tower are excellent. Though it is possible to continue further south-west beyond point 156m, the ground falls away ever more precipitously, and the increased exposure means it is not recommended.

Back at the signal tower the route turns north, following a signed, peaty path along the edge of the cliff. A short, steep climb brings you to the highest point of the route, where the precipice reaches 230m high near the summit of Foiltagarriff. There is another stunning view from here back to the south-west, across the signal tower and all the way to Bray Head, with the Skellig Islands still visible in the ocean beyond.

Continue to follow the waymarks north along the cliff for a short distance, then swing sharply east and begin the return leg of the walk. Though you must now leave the most dramatic scenery behind, there are still magnificent views across the length of Valentia Island into the rugged heart of the Iveragh Peninsula.

The descent begins gradually but becomes steeper as you head towards a fence. Turn right in front of the fence, and follow it gently downhill for a few hundred metres. A final turn south-east brings you back to the track you used on the outward part of the walk. Turn left onto the track, then recross the stile. Follow the road for the final few metres back to the car park.

Walkers on the final part of the descent.

ROUTE 26

Bolus Head

Grade:	3
Time:	2½–3½ hours
Distance:	9km (5½ miles)
Ascent:	270m (890ft)
Map:	OSi 1:50,000 sheet 83

Climb along sheer cliffs to reach a fabulous viewpoint at the top of 284m-high Bolus Head in County Kerry.

Start & Finish: The route starts and finishes at a small parking area at Allagheemore, on the northern side of the Bolus Head Peninsula (grid reference: V388650). Access to the area is from the R566, approximately 9km south of Portmagee. The walk is signed from this junction. Follow the minor road south for approximately 2.5km to reach a parking area on the left. The lay-by is marked by a walk information board, and provides parking space for several cars.

The largest, highest and boldest of all of the headlands on the Iveragh Peninsula, Bolus Head is home to a rewarding loop walk. The coastal scenery includes stunning views over St Finan's Bay, the Skellig Islands and the vertiginous cliffs of both Ducalla and Bolus Heads.

The route is part of the national loop walk network, and is signed throughout. The first and final sections follow firm roads and tracks, but the middle stretch takes you along informal footpaths, over open hillside and along the top of steep cliffs. Please take care near the edge, and avoid the route altogether in strong winds.

As well as the Atlantic scenery, the route passes several sites of historic interest. Many of these have a military theme. There are the remains of an old barracks and lookout post at the top of the headland itself, and the route starts and finishes beside a memorial to the eleven-man crew of a US Navy Liberator. This aeroplane is believed to have gone down near the Skellig Islands on 27 February 1944, during the Second World War. Reports from the lighthouse staff on Skellig Michael, which was permanently manned at that time, suggest the aircraft crashed into the upper part of the island. However, no signs of either the plane wreckage nor the remains of the crew were ever found.

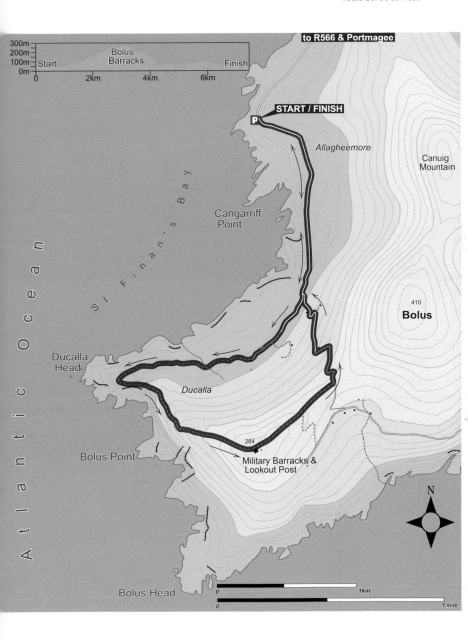

300m
200m
100m
0m
Start
0 2km 4km 6km
Bolus
Barracks
Finish

to R566 & Portmagee

START / FINISH
P

Allagheemore

Canuig
Mountain

St. Finan's Bay

Cangarriff
Point

410
Bolus

Ducalla
Head

Ducalla

Bolus Point

284

Military Barracks &
Lookout Post

N

Atlantic Ocean

Bolus Head

0 1km
0 1 mile

Looking north across St Finan's Bay from Ducalla Head.

The Walk

From the parking area, begin by following the road south down a short, steep hill. Already there are fine views across the surf-fringed peninsula of Cangarriff Point, and over the patchwork of bog and pasture sloping down to Ducalla Head. It is also possible to see most of the route from here, but do not be deceived: completing the circuit takes longer than you might think.

The road remains flat for a few hundred metres as it passes beneath the sombre slopes of Canuig Mountain (381m), then begins to climb steadily. Roughly 1.5km from the start you reach a Y-junction. The loop will return along the left-hand lane here, but for now, keep right and follow this road south-west towards Ducalla Head.

The road quickly becomes a track, which ends at an abandoned farmhouse. Cross a stile beside a gate and pass around the right side of the building. Now turn right and look carefully for a series of waymarks in the tussocks ahead. There is an informal path to follow, though it takes a meandering route and is not always obvious underfoot, and it can be muddy and wet in places.

After a gradual descent, cross a stream and begin to climb diagonally across the steepening slopes ahead. Already there are fine views across St Finan's Bay to the north. You arrive suddenly at the cliff edge just east of Ducalla Head. The route turns left here, but it is also worth making a small detour along the cliffs to the right to peer down sheer cliffs into the cove below.

The crumbling sandstone cliffs beneath Bolus Point, seen from Ducalla Head.

When you're ready, return to the official route and climb steeply – and spectacularly – along the cliff edge. This brings you to a magnificent viewpoint looking south along the crumbling sandstone cliffs to Bolus Point. There is a brief respite as you continue past the remains of an old stone shelter, but the gradient soon kicks up again as you make the final climb onto the flat summit of Bolus Head.

Bolus Head is marked by a concrete lookout post from the Second World War, and the stone ruins of some military barracks dating from the Napoleonic era. Unfortunately, it is not possible to inspect the barracks at close hand as they are fenced off, but you can get close enough to appreciate just what a cold and unrelenting base this must have been for anybody posted here, especially during the winter months. Hopefully the views provided some compensation for the exposure and isolation. The panorama to the north-west is especially impressive, across St Finan's Bay to Puffin Island, and beyond to the distant silhouettes of the Dingle Peninsula and Blasket Islands.

The route now turns inland and begins the

The military barracks at the summit of Bolus Head date from the Napoleonic era.

View north from the top of Bolus Head.

return leg, following a fence north-east in the direction of the 410m hill of Bolus. It is possible to climb almost to the summit of this hill as a short detour from the official route, though a fence not far from the summit precludes reaching the top itself.

The official route takes you to a peaty col beneath Bolus, then turns left and joins a track. Follow the track as it makes its way downhill through a series of pleasant switchbacks, then joins a sealed road near a farmhouse. Descend steeply along the road to reach the Y-junction you passed on the outward leg of the walk. Turn right here and follow the road for 1.5km back to the start.

Sheep grazing beside the descent track.

UNITED STATES NAVY LIBERATOR "63939"
FLEET AIR WING 7, VB-110 SQUADRON
CRASHED OFF SKELLIG MICHAEL
FEBRUARY 27th 1944

J. L. WILLIAMS	–	LOUISIANA
C. W. QUIGLE	–	INDIANA
K. L. BOWMAN	–	KANSAS
E. W. LIBBY	–	MASSACHUSETTS
J. T. FLENER	–	ILLINOIS
J. A. HUFFMAN	–	VIRGINIA
E. G. WILLIS	–	N. CAROLINA
G. E. DAVISON	–	MICHIGAN
J. E. McLAUGHLIN	–	WASHINGTON
H. C. CROW	–	TEXAS
M. J. OLSON	–	MINNESOTA

NÁ DHEANIS DHEARMAD
LEST WE FORGET

THE WARPLANE RESEARCH GROUP OF IRELAND
AUGUST 18th 1990

Memorial to the US Navy Liberator at the start of the route.

Derrynane Mass Path

Grade:	3
Time:	2½–3½ hours
Distance:	8km (5 miles)
Ascent:	180m (590ft)
Map:	OSi 1:50,000 sheet 84

Explore pristine beaches, a tidal island and a historic Mass path at the southern reaches of the Ring of Kerry.

Start & Finish: The walk starts and finishes at the car park for Derrynane Dunes Nature Trail, around 200m east of the main car park for Derrynane House (grid reference: V534587). Begin by following the N70 to the village of Caherdaniel. From here, take the minor road west from the centre of the village, following signs for Derrynane House. Veer left at a junction after 1.5km, then turn immediately left to reach the car park.

The Ring of Kerry is one of Ireland's most popular tourist destinations, and it doesn't take long to appreciate why. Stunning beaches combine with a rugged, mountainous interior to create some extraordinarily pretty scenes. In the midst of it all – and in many ways exemplifying the best of it – is this coastal circuit near Derrynane.

The route is relatively short yet immensely varied. A long, sandy beach, a rocky Mass path, country lanes and the Kerry Way all provide passage along various sections. An ascent of a modest mountain shoulder adds wonderful views over numerous offshore islets, with the distinctive outline of the Skellig Islands prominent amongst them. At low tide you can also cross a sandy isthmus to reach Abbey Island, where the remains of a 1,300-year-old abbey await exploration.

The route starts and finishes within the grounds of Derrynane National Historic Park, and it makes sense to add a visit to Derrynane House at the end of the walk. The house is the ancestral home of Daniel O'Connell, 'The Liberator', who was born in 1775. O'Connell is credited with mobilising the Irish people into their first mass movement, thus beginning the process by which Ireland eventually gained its independence.

O'Connell demanded that the state's many anti-Catholic laws be removed. His efforts eventually earned him a prison sentence. He is considered one of the heroes of modern Ireland, and the village of Caherdaniel is named in his honour.

Derrynane House is open to visitors daily from May to September and less frequently during the winter, and entry costs €4. For more information, contact 066 947 5113.

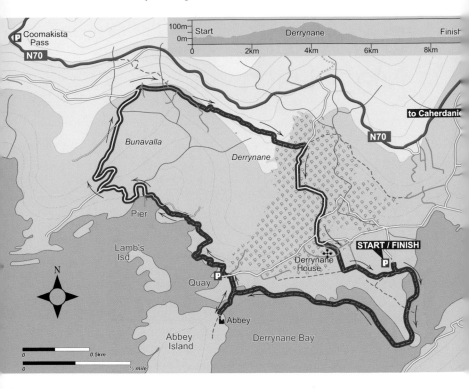

The Walk

From the beach end of the car park, follow a footpath signed as Derrynane Dunes Nature Trail. The path leads south to a trail junction; turn left here to reach the edge of the expansive sand flats that border the Coomnahorna River estuary. The slopes of Eagle Hill rise on the opposite bank of the river, while wading birds can often be seen picking over the spoils in the shallows below.

Turn right and follow the riverbank to the back of the dunes, then continue ahead along a smaller footpath that weaves through the sandhills. Descend to the firm sand of the beach and turn right. Follow the beach north-west for more than 1km, passing several rock outcrops along the way. The sheltering arms of the bay mean the turquoise waters are normally quite calm, and this is a popular spot with families during the summer. Nonetheless, warnings on the rocks indicate that some places can be treacherous for swimmers.

At the end of the beach, your onward route depends on the state of the tide. At low tide, simply continue along the sand, sweeping south at the end of the bay to reach Abbey Island. Here you will find the evocative ruins of Derrynane Abbey, believed to have been founded by St Finian around the eighth century. The roofless stone buildings are surrounded by graves, one of which belongs to Mary O'Connell, wife of Daniel O'Connell. Keep an eye on the sea level while you explore the site, however, as the neck of sand connecting the island to the mainland is covered at high tide. When you're ready, cross back to the end of the main beach and head left. Follow an access path and then a short section of tarmac to reach Abbey Island pier and car park at the end of the road.

The route spends more than 1km crossing the firm sands of Derrynane Strand.

At high tide the water covers the western end of the beach, making Abbey Island inaccessible. You will be forced off the sand soon after a yellow lifeguard hut. Cross the back of the beach to a parking area, then walk along the access road to a junction. Turn left here, following signs to Abbey Island. At the end of the road you arrive at Abbey Island pier and car park, rejoining walkers on the low-tide route.

The next part of the route follows an old Mass path along a rougher section of coastline. The path begins 50m up the road from the pier, and is marked by a waymarking post and a set of steps in a stone wall. Follow the trail around the back of a building, and you will soon find yourself weaving between seams of rock and climbing several flights of ancient stone steps, surrounded all the while by a wonderfully wild coastal landscape. It is easy to imagine locals in centuries gone by, filing along the path on their way to celebrate Mass at the abbey.

Descend to a stony cove and continue along the shore. Ignore two right turns, following the path across a stile to join a track. Turn left

Walking above Derrynane Strand, near Abbey Island.

The ruins of Derrynane Abbey, which was founded by St Finian in the eighth century.

here and pass around the back of another small beach to reach a pier, where a minor road leads uphill to the right. Follow this lane as it climbs steeply up the hillside, keeping right at a junction. Around 1.5km from the pier you arrive at a sharp left-hand switchback, with a prominent signpost at the corner that indicates the route of the Kerry Way.

Turn right here, following the Kerry Way east along a small lane. The marker posts of this 215km route will guide you for the next 1.5km. Cross a metal gate and stile, then watch for a left turn 200m later, where a footpath begins to climb across open ground. A short, sharp ascent brings you to the top of a spur of Farraniaragh Mountain, with the extra elevation affording fine coastal views that include the Beara Peninsula to the south.

Looking across Derrynane Bay, from near Abbey Island.

The Mass path includes several flights of ancient stone steps that weave between rock outcrops.

On the eastern side of the spur, the trail descends along a stony woodland path to reach a minor road. The Kerry Way continues straight ahead, but this route turns right along the tarmac. Descend for 1km to a junction. Continue straight ahead here, following signs for Derrynane Harbour. Around 100m beyond the junction, the white gateposts of Derrynane House appear on the left. Pass through these and follow the lane past ornamental gardens to reach the house itself. If you have time, this is your opportunity to explore the house and grounds in more detail.

To return to the start, pass round the house to reach the flagpoles at the seaward side of the building. Now follow a grassy path south to a wooden gate, which provides access to the back of the dunes. Turn left here onto a path signed with the low markers of the Dunes Nature Trail. Follow this route across a coastal meadow to a thicket of trees. Turn left at a junction beside the trees to return to the car park where the route began.

ROUTE 28

Dursey Island

Grade:	3
Time:	3½–4½ hours
Distance:	11.5km (7 miles)
Ascent:	410m (1,350ft)
Map:	OSi 1:50,000 sheet 84

A cable car journey and fine ridge-top walking make this signed route a memorable experience.

Start & Finish: The route starts and finishes at the cable car station on Dursey Island (grid reference: V505415). Begin by heading to Castletownbere on the southern side of the Beara Peninsula. From here head west along the R572 for 22km, following signs for Dursey Island. The mainland cable car station is located at the end of the road, and has a large car park. The cable car operates daily except in high winds. It runs continuously from 9.30 a.m. to 8 p.m. from June to September, and has scheduled service periods during the rest of the year. See www.durseyisland.ie for the full timetable. The cabin holds six people, the crossing takes about ten minutes, and return passage costs €8.

Dursey Island is a Signature Discovery Point of the Wild Atlantic Way. It measures 6.5km long but never more than 1.5km wide, and is a hilly island, a continuation of the Slieve Muckish Mountains that grace the southern end of the Beara Peninsula. Yet Dursey is set adrift, separated from the mainland by a channel 250m wide. Not far, you might think. Yet the sound has a strong tidal race and a rocky reef in the centre, and is treacherous even in calm conditions.

The solution for people wanting to access the island is to climb aboard Ireland's only cable car, indeed one of the only cable cars in Europe that spans an ocean chasm. The experience of swooping across the channel some 250m above the water is unique, and a fitting introduction to an atmospheric island.

Despite its apparent isolation, Dursey has been inhabited since the Bronze Age. It features in ancient Irish mythologies, and its name comes from the Norse word *Thjorsey*, meaning Bull Island, which was given by the Vikings when they operated a slave depot here around 1000 AD. A community has survived on Dursey until very recently; the population numbered more than 200 people in 1901, though just six remained at the turn of the millennium.

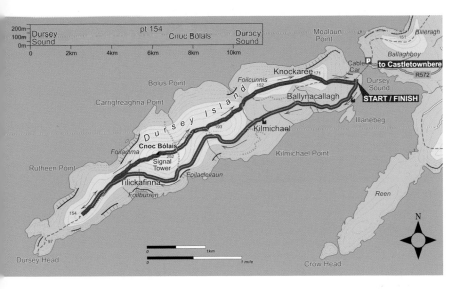

For walkers, Dursey is a memorable place to explore. Its sometimes poignant history combines with an open ridgeline and stunning coastal scenery to make a great day out. The island has a marked walking route, which is both a national loop walk and part of the long-distance Beara Way. The signs take you along the old road to the western tip of the island, then climbs over the hilltops on the return. The off-road terrain consists mainly of short grass and heather, but boots are recommended for the occasional patch of bog and rock.

Cable car across Dursey Sound with the mainland in the background. COURTESY WWW.ADRIANHENDROFF.COM

The Walk

The route is signed throughout with a mixture of purple and yellow arrows. From the cable car station, begin by following the road that contours along the southern side of the island. The road itself is a single-track lane, often endowed with a wide strip of grass down the middle. The island's pier lies on the shore 300m south of the cable car, followed by some stone

155

Signposts beside Dursey cable car station.
COURTESY WWW.ADRIANHENDROFF.COM

ruins that are the remains of St Mary's Abbey, an old monastery and graveyard.

Just beyond this, the islet of Illanebeg once held a castle belonging to the O'Sullivan Beare family, who controlled the Beara Peninsula for 300 years. A drawbridge spanned the gap to Dursey. In 1602 Queen Elizabeth's forces stormed the fort, aided by an O'Sullivan kinsman from a rival faction. More than 300 islanders were killed, many reputedly thrown off the cliffs in what became known as the Dursey Massacre. Some of the bodies were buried in the O'Sullivan Beare vault, which can still be seen in the graveyard of the old monastery.

After 1km you pass the hamlet of Ballynacallagh, the first of three largely abandoned settlements on the island. The patchwork of stone-walled fields surrounding the road is testament to a more productive past. The second village, Kilmichael, comes less than a kilometre further on. A

Descending towards Dursey Head, with The Calf (left), The Cow and Bull Rock (right) visible out to sea. COURTESY WWW.ADRIANHENDROFF.COM

Looking north from southern end of Dursey Island. Courtesy www.adrianhendroff.com

pile of rock near the start of the village is actually a ruined church thought to have been founded by monks from the Skellig Islands.

Keep left at a fork and continue along the road for another 3km, passing the third hamlet of Tilickafinna on the way. The return route turns right shortly before the end of the road, but it is worth continuing along a grassy track at least as far as the rise ahead. This 154m summit provides fine views over the western tip of Dursey, with its three attendant islets, The Cow, The Calf and Bull Rock. Bull Rock, the northernmost island, holds a large sea arch, and was once believed to be a doorway to the otherworld. Today it is home to a large gannet colony.

The history of lighthouses in the area is an interesting one. One was first constructed on The Calf in 1866, but was snapped in half by a storm just fifteen years later (the stump of the old tower can still be seen). A temporary beacon was constructed on Dursey Head, and the square stone walls of this building remain visible at the tip of the headland. This bought enough time for a new lighthouse to be built on Bull Rock, which began signalling in 1889 and is still operational today.

It is possible to continue all the way down, past point 97m, to the western tip of Dursey, but many people are happy to turn around at point 154m. From here, retrace your steps back to the end of the road. Veer left here, following a marked path up the ridge towards Cnoc Bólais, the highest point on the island.

Near the top of the slope, to the left of the path, the remains of the word 'Eire' can be seen written in white stones on the ground. This served as a navigational marker for pilots during the Second World War. The 252m summit holds a trig point, and a remarkably intact signal tower dating from 1804. Incredible views stretch in all directions. The panorama includes the jagged outcrops of the Skellig Islands to the north-west, the Iveragh Peninsula to the north, the Mizen and Sheep's Head peninsulas to the south, and the undulating spine of Dursey and Beara to the east.

Descend east from the summit, crossing a stile and joining a grassy track that leads down into a broad col. A gentle climb brings you over the next rise, then a steeper descent leads to a choice of routes in the saddle below.

To keep on the official route, veer right here, following signs for the cable car. A series of old tracks carries you around the fields and back to the road at Ballynacallagh. Turn left and follow the road for 1km to return to the cable car station.

Alternatively you can continue along the ridge from the saddle, climbing across open ground, past point 152m to Knockaree. The ridge narrows enjoyably here, with a precipitous drop to the north and rocky outcrops underfoot. This option provides a wilder finale, prolonging the views and adding a bird's-eye perspective across Dursey Sound. From the summit of Knockaree, descend east along an informal path to return to the cable car station.

Bere Island

Coomastooka Circuit		Lighthouse Loop	
Grade:	3	**Grade:**	3
Time:	4–5 hours	**Time:**	2½–3½ hours
Distance:	13km (8 miles)	**Distance:**	8km (5 miles)
Ascent:	350m (1,150ft)	**Ascent:**	230m (750ft)
Map:	OSi 1:50,000 sheet 84	**Map:**	OSi 1:50,000 sheet 84

A choice of two signed routes explore the rugged hills and open coastline of this friendly island off the Cork coast.

Start & Finish: Both walks start and finish at the ferry pier on the north-western tip of Bere Island (grid reference: V685445). Ferries leave the mainland from Castletownbere harbour, at a slipway opposite the SuperValu shop. Services are operated by **Bere Island Ferries** (Tel: 086 2423 140; www. bereislandferries.com). There are between four and seven crossings daily, all year round, so it is perfectly feasible to complete your walk as part of a day trip. Return passage costs €8 and the crossing takes just ten minutes.

Lying just south of the Beara Peninsula at the mouth of Bantry Bay, Bere Island measures 10km long by 3km wide, and has a population of just over 200. It is separated from the mainland by a channel that narrows to 400m, and its rugged landscape is a continuation of the mountainous upland that covers the mainland. The island's walks cross wild and hilly terrain, yet have the advantage of being fully signed, and provide a wonderful overview of the unspoiled scenery of the area.

Two different routes are described here. The longer route, the Coomastooka Circuit, begins by climbing along 4km of road to reach the centre of the island. A series of tracks and footpaths then lead past the island's highest point, before an open descent brings you to the picturesque lighthouse at Ardnakinna Point. The shorter option follows the western half of this route, missing the views across the eastern side of the island but still visiting the lighthouse.

The island's location at the entrance to Bantry Bay has imbued it with strategic importance over the centuries, and it has a long history of human habitation. The oldest monument viewed on the route dates to

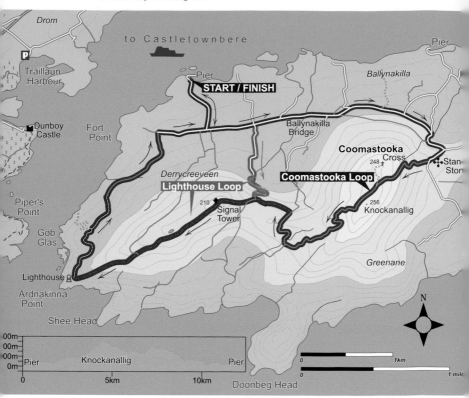

the Bronze Age, and there are many other buildings stemming from the island's military significance in the eighteenth and nineteenth centuries. Two Martello towers, a signal tower and an old military road are all features originating from this era.

Both routes described are offshoots of the 196km-long Beara Way. Frequent waymarking posts mean navigation is a relatively simple affair, though you should avoid walking if the cloud is down across the hills. The mixture of quiet laneway, mountain track and rough footpath provides plenty of variety underfoot, but good boots are essential for the open sections, where the terrain is rough and rugged.

The Walk

Coomastooka Circuit

From the ferry slipway, head around the harbour and walk uphill along the road. After 700m you arrive at a T-junction. Turn left here, following a

Walking along the track near Coomastooka, with Bantry Bay ahead.

marker post signed 'Beara Way to Rerin Village'. Follow the road as it climbs gradually east, keeping straight ahead at all junctions and passing the island's heritage centre and hotel.

After 2.5km you arrive at a T-junction. Turn right here, still climbing towards the spine of the island. After 400m turn right again, and the views suddenly open out over the hills and villages on the eastern side of Bere. Various structures can be seen marking the summits; the largest two are Martello towers, circular artillery stations built in 1805 to defend against a French invasion. These are all that remain of four Martello towers once located on the island. In a field to the left of the road you will also notice a gallán, or standing stone, a 3m-tall Bronze Age monument that stands at the exact centre point of the island.

Pass round a corner and look out for a grassy track on the right, barred by a metal gate. A Beara Way post directs you over the stile beside the gate. A large, white cross is visible at the top of the rise ahead, and this is the first goal of the route.

Follow the track uphill across open ground. Climb almost to the top of the hill, then turn left at a track junction. This brings you to the cross and an adjacent wind turbine, which mark the 248m summit of Coomastooka. The hill makes a wonderful vantage point, providing great views across most of Bere Island and well as the Beara Peninsula to the north. The cross was erected in 1950, and Mass is still celebrated here once a year on the August bank holiday weekend.

Retrace your steps to the junction, then turn right. As you pass over a rise, another fine vista is suddenly revealed to the south, across Bantry Bay

Descending towards Ardnakinna Lighthouse at the south-western tip of the island.

to the Sheep's Head Peninsula. Follow the track as it makes a zigzagging descent through the hummocks. A ruined signal tower is now visible on the top of the hill to the west, and this is your next goal.

Turn right at the next track junction and cross back over the spine of the island. Shortly after you begin to descend, look out for a marker post directing you left, onto a rough footpath above a fence. Contour across the hillside, then turn left onto another track. This brings you to a three-way junction marked by a tall metal signpost. This is where you join the shorter Lighthouse Loop, and both routes continue in tandem from this point on.

Follow the track uphill from the metal sign for 100m, then turn right onto a footpath. Climb steeply to reach the ruined stone tower at the top of the hill. This was once a two-storey signal tower dating from the Napoleonic era, but was first struck by lightning in 1959 then blown down during a storm in 1964, leaving just the low walls that are visible today.

The descent from the signal tower to the lighthouse follows a footpath across open, rugged hillside studded with rock outcrops. Frequent marker posts and splashes of yellow paint keep you heading in the right direction. The lighthouse itself is located relatively low down, and remains hidden from sight until you're almost on top of it. A remote, single white tower set against a beautiful backdrop, this is an atmospheric place to linger on a good day. The lighthouse itself dates from 1965 and warns of treacherous rocks around Piper's Point below.

Fishing boats in the harbour, beside the ferry slipway at the start and finish of the route.

When you're ready, head north along the grassy access track, which began life as a nineteenth-century military road. Descend through several hairpin bends, then watch out for a right turn onto a rough path. This brings you across the hillside, past good views over the channel to the ruins of Dunboy Castle and the restored Puxley mansion, which date from the sixteenth and eighteenth centuries respectively.

Follow the path to the end of a track, which is barred by a metal gate. Cross the adjacent stile, then continue past two further stiles. When you reach a T-junction, turn right onto a tarmac lane. Follow the lane for 500m, then turn left onto the road signed for the ferry. Retrace your initial steps back down the hill to the harbour, where with luck your ferry will be waiting.

Lighthouse Loop

This loop begins in the same way as the Coomastooka Circuit. Head up the road from the pier to a T-junction. The Lighthouse Loop is signed to the right here, but it is actually better walked in a clockwise direction, so turn left instead. Follow the road for 500m, then turning right onto a narrow lane. Climb past several houses to reach a metal gate at the end of the road. Pass over a stile beside the gate and continue ahead along a stony track, now surrounded by open mountainside. The track zigzags uphill and brings you to a three-way junction marked by a tall metal signpost. This is where you rejoin the Coomastooka Circuit. Turn right at the junction and follow the instructions for that route all the way back to the harbour.

The Sheep's Head

Lighthouse Loop	
Grade:	3
Time:	1–2 hours
Distance:	4km (2½ miles)
Ascent:	150m (490ft)
Map:	OSi 1:50,000 sheet 88

The Poet's Way	
Grade:	3
Time:	3½–4½ hours
Distance:	12.5km (8 miles)
Ascent:	320m (1,050ft)
Map:	OSi 1:50,000 sheet 88

Wild scenery and fantastic views await at the tip of this remote peninsula in west Cork, with a choice of long and short routes on offer.

Start & Finish: Both routes start and finish at a car park at the western tip of the Sheep's Head Peninsula (grid reference: V733340). To access the area, follow the road along the southern side of the peninsula, passing through the village of Kilcrohane. Now follow signs for 'Sheep's Head', continuing for a further 9km to the end of the road. The car park has a toilet block and café, which are open during summer months only.

Lough Akeen, near the tip of Sheep's Head.

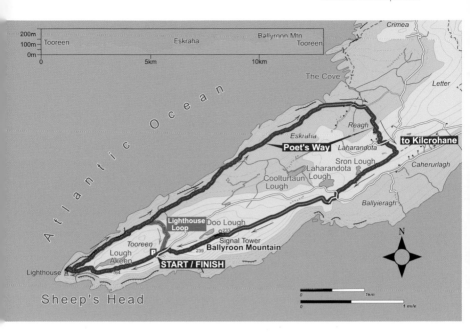

The Sheep's Head is the most isolated peninsula in south-west Ireland, and best described by the closing line of Seamus Heaney's poem 'The Peninsula', which has been adopted as an epithet for the area. The line reads, 'Water and ground in their extremity'. This motto is particularly relevant to the very tip of the headland, where a wild and rather primeval atmosphere pervades.

Walker looking across Lough Akeen.

Two different circuits are described here, both fully signed, and both exploring the final few kilometres of land before the promontory finally concedes to the sea. The coastal views are wonderful throughout, with Mizen Head dominating to the south and the Beara Peninsula rising across Bantry Bay to the north.

The short option – the Lighthouse Loop – is marked by blue arrows. It circumnavigates the far western tip of the peninsula, encompassing what is arguably the most impressive section of

Sunset over Bantry Bay from the Sheep's Head.

the longer route. The Poet's Way is signed by red arrows. It begins by covering the same ground, but extends further east along the flanks of the headland, giving a better overall impression of the area and including an enjoyable traverse of Ballyroon Mountain, whose summit provides the modest highpoint at 239m.

Both routes are offshoots of the 88km-long Sheep's Head Way. They follow obvious footpaths throughout, and take advantage of the stiles, footbridges and marker posts that furnish the long-distance trail. The terrain underfoot is rugged and undulating, consisting of thick moorland grass punctuated by outcrops of rock. Good boots are recommended for both routes.

The Walk

The short Lighthouse Loop and longer Poet's Way follow the same route for the first 3km of the walk. From the car park, begin by heading west along the road for another 50m, then veer right onto a gravel footpath. This trail carries you easily across a delightful expanse of wild and rugged upland, then passes along the southern shore of scenic Lough Akeen.

At the end of the lake, cross a wooden bridge over a marshy ditch, then make a final short climb to reach a helicopter landing pad encircled with white stones. Sheep's Head Lighthouse lies partway down the slope to the right of the helipad – you can access the building by descending a flight

A variety of signs mark the route – this one is for the Sheep's Head Way.

of concrete steps with a red handrail. The lighthouse is just 7m tall and was constructed in 1968 to mark the entrance of Bantry Bay.

When you are ready, return to the helipad and turn left onto the path that runs along the northern side of the peninsula. There are several wet hollows here that you will either have to skirt around, or avoid by climbing a short distance up to the left. Continue along the top of some 100m-high cliffs. The scenery is impressive here, but care is needed near the edge.

A gradual climb brings you to a trail junction. The Lighthouse Loop turns right here, following the blue arrows across rock-studded ground and back to the car park. To stay on the Poet's Way, keep straight ahead along the coast. Rocks become less frequent now, and you pass through swathes of thick grass. Descend to a pretty sea inlet, where encroaching tides have chiselled a narrow gash into the rock and created two natural arches. A waterfall streams into the top of the inlet, and the whole effect is quite charming.

Continue over several grassy hummocks, then the hamlet of Eskraha comes into sight ahead. Cross a stile beside a gate and follow a track beneath the buildings. Turn left onto a minor road, then 100m later, turn right beside a tall metal signpost. Pass over another stile and climb steeply alongside some fields.

This brings you to the spine of the peninsula, where you join a lane and follow it left for 50m. Now turn right again, following another footpath across open, rugged terrain. Soon the trail turns right and begins to contour south-west across the hillside. You may have to skirt around the edge of the occasional wet patch here. Negotiate several more stiles and continue past two small loughs before descending to a road.

Turn left along the tarmac for 20m, then turn right onto a lane. As you pass some houses the lane dwindles to a track, then shrinks to a footpath as you begin the ascent of Ballyroon Mountain.

The route climbs along the apex of a ridge, with boulders and rock outcrops pushing through the grass below. The gradient is relatively benign, and fine views span both sides of the peninsula. Once you reach the summit ridge, the first landmark is a pile of rocks that is actually a ruined signal tower dating from the early nineteenth century. The tower originally stood three storeys high and was intact until 1990, when it was blown down in a gale.

Continue ahead to reach the official summit, which is marked by a trig point and fabulous views both north and south across the Beara, Iveragh and Mizen Head peninsulas. The descent takes you past a square, concrete building, which was used as a lookout post during the Second World War. Continue downhill from here to return to the car park where the route began.

The route climbs along the apex of the ridge as it crosses Ballyroon Mountain.